Contact your Spirit Guides

to enrich your life

Other Foulsham books by Cassandra Eason

Cassandra's books are available from all good bookshops or direct from www.foulsham.com.

Cassandra Eason's Complete Book of Spells (0-572-03001-0)

Cassandra Eason's Modern Book of Dream Interpretation (0-572-03081-9)

Chakra Power for Healing and Harmony (0-572-02749-4)

Crystal Healing (0-572-02735-4)

Crystals Talk to the Woman Within (0-572-02613-7)

Discover Your Past Lives (0-572-02198-4)

Every Woman a Witch (0-572-02223-9)

Fragrant Magic (0-572-02939-X)

I Ching Divination for Today's Woman (0-572-01895-9)

Magic Spells for a Happy Life (0-572-02827-X)

Practical Guide to Witchcraft and Magick Spells (0-572-02704-4)

Psychic Power of Children and How to Deal With It (0-572-03061-4)

Psychic Suburbia (0-572-02036-8)

Smudging and Incense-burning (0-572-02737-0)

Cassandra Eason can be contacted through her website at www.cassandraeason.co.uk

contact your
Spirit
Guides
to enrich your life

cassandra eason

quantum
LONDON • NEW YORK • TORONTO • SYDNEY

quantum

An imprint of W. Foulsham & Co. Ltd
The Publishing House, Bennetts Close, Cippenham, Slough,
Berkshire, SL1 5AP, England

ISBN 0-572-03128-9

First published by Bokförlaget New Page AB, Sweden with the title *The Key to Spirit Guides*. Copyright © 2004 av Cassandra Eason; copyright © 2004 Bokförlaget New Page AB. Published by arrangement with Tönnheim Literary Agency, Sweden

Cover illustration by Jurgen Ziewe

Illustrations by Ruth Murray and Hayley Francesconi

A CIP record for this book is available from the British Library

Disclaimer: The exercises in this book are intended for increasing self-awareness. However, if you have recently experienced psychological problems or are taking prescribed medication you should seek professional medical advice before practising meditation. Neither the editors of W. Foulsham & Co. Ltd nor the author nor the publisher take responsibility for any possible consequences from any treatment, procedure, test, exercise, action or application of medication or preparation by any person reading or following the information in this book. The publication of this book does not constitute the practice of medicine, and this book does not attempt to replace any diet or instructions from your doctor. The author and publisher advise the reader to check with a doctor before administering any medication or undertaking any course of treatment or exercise.

Printed in Great Britain by Creative Print & Design (Wales), Ebbw Vale

Contents

Introduction

We are all guided and protected by spiritual beings from the moment our own spirit enters our earthly body until we return to the spiritual world after death. Some people are not aware of these protectors from higher dimensions or choose not to admit them into their lives. They can still live happy, fulfilled lives drawing on earthly support and their own resources. Even so, this book may be of interest to add awareness that we do all have spiritual natures and keep our connection with higher realms, even though spirituality may be expressed entirely through everyday living.

Many of us may have forgotten our earlier childhood connections with the spiritual world, which often touches the material one, and would love to know more of the worlds we occasionally glimpse in a beautiful, natural place or in a church, temple, sacred site or cathedral.

For in childhood we are more open to angels, fairies, nature spirits, kind, departed family members who watch over us, and small invisible friends with whom we play as easily as earthly companions. But as we grow older and our lives become more demanding, frantic and filled with the constant noise, information and stimulation of the modern technological world, so our spiritual horizons may shrink.

Yet our spiritual companions do not leave us, but still gently guide us away from dangers. They may send signs to make us stop and take notice when we are about to make an unwise decision or act thoughtlessly. This may be a sudden stirring of the breeze on a windless day bringing a shower of petals, a white feather that floats down in front of our nose (a common angel communication), the fragrance of a deceased grandmother or the smell of the tobacco of a much-loved, departed grandfather at a time when we need their wise counsel.

For spiritual companions take many forms, from a deceased relative who appears at the birth of a baby to darting nature spirits in long grass, from a wise teacher from an ancient culture to a full-blown archangel. You may have seen these guides in a dream and wondered about their significance in your life (they usually appear when you have a big decision to make). In waking hours you may have felt a touch as light as gossamer or a sudden warmth or sense of being cared for when you were anxious.

Rarely will your angel or guide manifest in front of you without warning. They always wait for you to ask them into your life and would never show themselves if it would spook you.

Spirit guides and guardians enrich our lives in all kinds of ways if we allow them to draw close in those quiet moments when we are sitting by candle- or firelight, or walking silently through a park or the countryside in the early morning.

I have suggested in this book ways of bringing the energies of spiritual protectors into the everyday world in a positive, safe way to make it richer and you more harmonious and in tune with yourself and the slower cycles of the natural world.

If you are sad, lonely, tired after a long journey or afraid, perhaps of flying in a plane or of the dark, your spiritual companions are there to fill you with peace. They will help you to make the most of your natural gifts at times of opportunity and to overcome obstacles when you feel you really cannot go on. They are your best friends, who always expect and think the best of you and, rather than taking you away from reality, help you to cope in any situation.

Above all, they encourage us to remain connected to our own spiritual nature and potential and to live with honesty and integrity. In this way we love and value ourselves, and so can make good connections with other people, even difficult ones.

In the following pages are descriptions of different kinds of spiritual companions and beliefs about the many levels of existence. But above all, this is a practical book to help you explore different spiritual energies and enjoy rituals and exercises as you travel the dimensions and bring what is of worth to you back to enrich the here and now.

1

Who are my spirit guides?

Spirit guides are benign spiritual beings who protect and guide us from infancy until we are ready to move into the next world. They may be childhood invisible friends, lifelong guardian angels or wise figures from another culture. Whatever they are and however they manifest, they are there to help us and help make our lives better.

Just as we are spiritual beings with a human form, so they are spiritual beings who have shed that human form. They are only different from us in that they are wiser and not constrained by physical time or space. Some of the more evolved spirit beings, who may draw close to teach or to heal us, may never have assumed human form, but nevertheless they understand human needs and weaknesses.

Spirit guides are not sitting around waiting for a mortal to call them, but when we need them they are always there. You may only sense them, or you may see a shadowy form or even a three-dimensional image with your inner or external eye, especially if it is your main spirit guide.

So think of your spirit guide as your best friend, who has your best interests at heart and can see the whole picture. You can talk to him or her in your mind at any time or anywhere. If you are not used to talking to your special guide or have not identified one and seek the wisdom of other guides, you can create a quiet, protected place for communication.

All these aspects will be explored in more depth throughout this book.

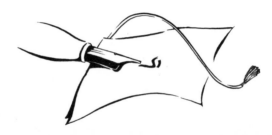

Spirit-guide manifestations

There are many ways in which you can encounter spirit guides and many ways in which they can help you.

Perhaps when you were a child you had an invisible friend who was always with you and took care of you when you were alone and scared. Any such friend who is associated with bringing comfort and security is a spirit guide.

For example, Myrtle was her eighties when she told me about her childhood angel friends who were, she said, no bigger than an adult finger. They came to play with Myrtle and talk to her when she was about four years old and living in colonial India. When Myrtle was seven she was sent across the world to England to a boarding school and only returned home once or twice a year. Her little angel friends stayed with her until she was settled and not homesick any more.

Many adults have experience of a guardian angel, similar to spirit guides. Spirit guides walk on Earth, angels through the stars and the heavens and both work together in their different ways to help you on your life path. The angel may have revealed a name or just be called 'my blue angel', which often refers to the colour ray that surrounds the angel.

Deceased family members also act as guides for the living. You may be aware of the perfume of a deceased grandmother when you feel worried or alone. This is not at all spooky but is comforting and a way of saying that love never dies and the essential person survives the death of the physical body. This may be the first adult contact with the spirit world and can open the door to encountering your personal spirit guide and guardian angel if you have not been aware of them, at least since childhood. You do not need to contact a spirit medium to enjoy connections with relatives who are no longer with us in this world, especially through dreams.

Though we have one lifelong guardian angel and a spirit guide, other guides and wise teachers appear according to our needs and the stage of life we have reached.

For example, a wise man or woman from another culture or age may appear to you regularly in dreams or guided visualisations and meditation and usually offers knowledge or a solution to life issues you may be facing at the time. He or she will act as your companion and teacher when you begin to explore other, higher realms and explore your own evolving spiritual potential.

Usually this wise figure comes from a culture with which you have a special spiritual connection or affinity, often one associated with great wisdom, such as Ancient Egypt, the Viking world, China or Native North America.

Even if you do not believe in past lives, since all life came out of East

10

Africa millions of years ago, we do all have common genetic links. Suddenly as we are walking round an ancient site or palace on holiday or are visiting a museum or art gallery, before us is the picture or a drawing of our dream guardian. I found my spirit guide on a painted statue called *The Scribe's Wife* in the museum in Cairo.

Much of the modern fascination with ancient gods and goddesses reflects the need we have to regain wisdom from ancient sources of beauty and knowledge. For example, a number of businesswomen in the Western as well as the Middle Eastern world take as their guide and protectress the Ancient Egyptian lion-headed goddess of fire Sekhmet, or Sekhet.

Occasionally a spirit guide may take the form of an animal or bird, or may be seen in their natural setting if they are a spirit of nature. These natural guides can help if our instincts have become blunted or we have lost our spontaneity.

Identifying our spirit guides

One theory is that our spirit guides are manifestations of our own evolved soul, or higher self, that we interpret in our minds and then externalise as a wise Native North American, a Chinese doctor or sage or a full-blown archangel. Through this wise part of ourselves we can access the well of universal wisdom from all times and places through our common genetic heritage.

However, evidence for countless case studies would suggest that spirit guides exist as independent entities. That is not to say that we do not use our own spiritual self for guidance, and it is also true that, whatever their source, spirit guides enrich our everyday as well as our spiritual world.

However, there may be specific causes for a personal lifetime guide to be linked emotionally to us. Our personal guide may be a member of our soul family, a group of souls who travel though different lifetimes together occupying different roles according to the lessons to be learned. Our spirit guide may be a particularly evolved member of this soul group who has chosen to remain on the spiritual plane for a while or permanently to guide the members of the soul family currently on Earth.

Alternatively, your permanent guide may be an ancestor from centuries before who has chosen to help you because you are following a similar life path to his or hers on Earth or share elements of their personality.

Sophia, who is an editor in New York, has been aware since childhood of the presence of her great-great-grandmother Eva from Poland and has been fascinated by her Polish past, though most of the family have lost the connection.

When Sophia recently visited Krakow, she learned more of Eva, who had left her family to seek a new life for herself and her young daughter in America after her husband had been killed. Sophia is also a single parent and has struggled to bring up her young daughter alone on the other side of America from her family in order to take up her present post in publishing work that enabled her to give her daughter a better start in life.

A small painting of Eva, found in the home of distant relatives in a small village outside Krakow, showed her to be a mirror image of Sophia. Most amazingly, in the picture Eva wore an amber necklace with a single cross of amber that Sophia had seen on her spirit guide. The necklace had, according to a distant cousin she became friendly with, been a family treasure that had to be sold to contribute towards the fare to America.

What can spirit guides do?

Before we begin to get in touch with spirit guides, let's learn a bit more about what spirit guides do and don't do.

Your spirit guide does not probe your thoughts or watch you 24 hours a day. He or she will never encroach on your privacy, whether you want to be alone with your lover or have a good scratch. It is up to you to make contact when you need their support and guidance.

The key to the relationship is trust. It is not going to work if you try to test your spirit guide to make them prove they are true and trustworthy. Think of them as a better part of yourself and you will not be tempted to make this mistake.

A spirit guide is always there to give you help and advice, so always keep in regular touch with them, but you should use your guide wisely and sparingly by asking for their help when you most need it. Try to sort out everyday issues yourself; spirit guides are not there to deal with the taxman or find you a parking space.

On the other hand, the major issues and decisions in your life should be shared with your spirit guide. Always contact them before you make a major decision, embark on a journey or make life changes. They will always try to alert you to danger or unwise actions, although don't forget that they are constrained by your free will – which includes the freedom to make mistakes – so they will not interfere. Nor can you hand over responsibility for decision-making. Sound out ideas with your guide and consider the advice carefully, but you must make the decision for yourself.

Your spirit guide is always your first port of call if you need healing for yourself or want to influence the healing of others. In these cases, your guides may direct you to specialist guides who are expert healers.

Spirit guides can also assist you if you want to know your grandma is all right in heaven. Indeed your spirit guide and your grandma's guide, who will still be supporting her in heaven, can together ease the channels of communication between Earth and the heavenly planes.

They can also help you to access higher planes through astral (mind) travel and through prayer. Your spirit guide will help to answer those prayers, not least by showing you ways you can answer them yourself.

For creative ventures, such as writing, music, art, drama or crafts, spirit guides will open your creative channels and guide you towards what the Greeks called the 'Muses' and Robert Graves, the twentieth-century historian and mythologist, called the 'White Goddess of Inspiration'.

Whenever you ask for cosmic help, remember that you are expected to pay it back. You can do this in any way that will help others or the environment. It could be feeding wild birds or being kind to another human being in need.

Finally, the affection of your spirit guide is total – without conditions. Even when you get everything wrong, they will patiently put you back on track without so much as an 'I told you so'.

2

Beginning communication with spirit guides

S pirit guides and other guardians, including angels, spontaneously communicate with us in a number of ways to let us know they are around. If you have not yet met any of your guides or angels, these signals may have seemed like a coincidence, a trick of the light or a blockage in your eardrum that causes you to hear bells. You may have noticed a dancing spark or balls of light in a dark room, smelled a beautiful floral scent or felt a touch as light as gossamer. When you were sad or anxious, a butterfly or beautiful moth may have appeared suddenly, even in winter, or a musical box that has not played for years suddenly started turning. All these are signs that your spirit guide is near. Your guardian angel uses similar channels and in time you will learn to know which one is with you. These signals, such as sound or light, are also a ready channel for you to indicate your readiness or need to talk to your guides.

In this chapter I am going to look at the preparations for contacting your spirit guides and how to do so in the right atmosphere of calm and security. You can also make a start in contacting your spirit guides.

Communicating through fragrance

Throughout the book I suggest a variety of techniques for safely encountering, communicating with and channelling wisdom and healing from your guides and angels.

One of the simplest and most positive ways of creating a protected atmosphere for spirit communication is by using timeless fragrances such as rose or lavender that are found worldwide and have been central to rituals through the ages. In ancient religions, fragrance, especially in the form of incense, carried the prayers of the faithful to the heavens because it was believed that fragrances were a gift of the gods so mortals might become more perfect by absorbing the scent.

The fragrances listed below will attract healing and wise spirits and automatically repel those who are less benign. Apple blossom, carnation, lavender and rose are especially protective against all negativity.

When you feel you are ready to start contacting your spirit guide, find a comfortable and calm place to relax. Choose your fragrance from the list; you can use the fresh flowers, incense, perfume or cologne or essential oils. Close your eyes. Slowly inhale the fragrance and ask quietly for the blessing you seek. Perhaps you simply want to meet them; perhaps you have a question to ask.

You may see in your mind the flower guardian surrounded by his or her own flowers or hear a soft voice offering reassurance and guidance. Allow the experience to take its own course. The spirit will then gradually fade away. The spiritual scent will remain long after the physical fragrance has faded, and you will know that you are being protected or uplifted in the hours and days ahead.

Protective fragrances

This information will help you when choosing your fragrances, both for this first encounter and for your future spirit-guide work.

Apple blossom: Work with apple blossom to contact guardians of health, healing, babies, children and fertility, or when you are emotionally exhausted or drained by the demands of others.

Carnation: Work with carnation to contact the guardians of the family and of family traditions, for help with older people and matters of justice or to restore confidence if you have suffered criticism or spite.

Geranium: Work with geranium to contact the guardians of quiet sleep and beautiful dreams or if you are very stressed or struggling against phobias or an addiction.

Hibiscus: Work with hibiscus to contact the guardians of creativity, especially in the arts or music, or if you have become depressed or feel life is passing you by.

Honeysuckle: Work with honeysuckle to contact the guardians of perseverance under difficulty, whether you are dealing with difficult people or going through a bad patch in a relationship or career.

Hyacinth: Work with hyacinth to contact the guardians of self-esteem, independence and strong identity, or if you are seeking a new beginning or to clear stagnation and inertia from your life.

Jasmine: Work with jasmine to contact the guardians of external and inner changes and transitions, or if you are seeking love or to develop your psychic gifts.

Lavender: Work with lavender to contact the guardians of healing, of the environment and animal welfare, or if you are gentle-natured, quietly spoken and are being ignored or badly treated.

Lilac: Work with lilac to contact the guardians of the home and domestic happiness, and for house moves and renovations, or if you feel you need to touch base when far away from home.

Lily: Work with lily to contact the guardians of inner strength and courage, or to resist emotional pressure and also to accept what cannot for now be changed.

Lotus or orchid: Work with lotus or orchid to contact the guardians of idealism, crusaders and of leaders and wise leadership, or when you need to speak out or act boldly in spite of opposition from the status quo.

Mimosa: Work with mimosa to contact the guardians of ancient wisdom and of spiritual, as opposed to material, fulfilment and to find and follow your unique destiny.

Neroli (orange blossom): Work with neroli to contact the guardians of serenity and permanence, and if you are seeking or pledging fidelity or loyalty of or to another.

Rose: Work with rose to contact the guardians of love, reconciliation and healing, or if you have suffered any kind of abuse or betrayal.

Violet: Work with violet to contact the guardians of what is hidden, both spiritual mysteries and secrets better not revealed, or for unrequited love and for supporting others in times of need.

Psychic protection

Psychic protection is like virus protection on your computer. If you follow basic rules – like not opening attachments you are not expecting or visiting sites with names that do not instinctively feel right – then your virus alert operates mainly in the background as a filter and a background shield.

With spirit-guide work in this book you will not be calling up spirits or entities at random. You will always be in control and aware, so no spirit form can or will negatively influence your body or mind. However, it is worth being aware and taking some simple precautions.

Most psychic protection is common sense. There are two types of negative spirit energies. One belongs to people who were mischief-makers in this world and are no better in the afterlife. The other belongs to lower spirit forms that may never have taken human form but just like to confuse mortals. In the same way that you would not invite people you did not like or trust into your home, you will rapidly come to recognise spirits that are less than helpful.

Rules for safe spirit-world contact

Your personal spirit guide and your other guardian spirits are, of course, kind and wise, but as with any new skill, you need to learn a basic safety routine so every encounter with the unseen world is positive and happy. You would not learn to drive a car without knowing basic road safety and it is the same with spirit encounters. There are number of simple, common-sense rules you should bear in mind when you are contacting the spirit world. They will ensure your psychic protection so that you can relax and enjoy the experience.

Remember at all times that you are only contacting benevolent spirits who are there to support, comfort and guide you. They will not try to influence your life; it is up to you whether you take their advice. If you feel any influence that you believe is not beneficial to you or you do not instinctively trust, it is not your spirit guide.

Never call up spirits with a ouija board or by inviting any spirits present to make themselves known at a séance. These are not the best ways to contact your personal spirit guide and can invite negative energies.

Some people who are particularly susceptible may find they are contacted out of the blue by apparently elevated entities. Be wary of them. It is unlikely that a deceased king, Princess Diana or the Buddha will suddenly manifest in your living room especially for your benefit. My late mother communicated with a spirit who said he was a member of the royal family and so she was very impressed. However, this entity slowly seemed to influence her mind more and more until at last she had to see the local priest. Whether psychic or psychological, apparently high-born spirits that flatter our ego need handling with caution. Also, be wary of any apparent spirit guide who promises to make you instantly rich or to get rid of somebody you don't like or to harm a person who is causing you problems. This is not how spirit guides work.

You can protect yourself from negative beings by not asking unwise questions. For example, don't request the answers to an examination in advance or ask how you can attract your best friend's partner. You may get what you want but it will not make you happy and, under cosmic laws, there would always be a price to pay. You can also be sure, in such cases, that you are not working with your spirit guide, as they would not answer such questions for you. It may be that a less well-intentioned spirit may be eavesdropping and see this weakness in you as a way to gain your attention.

Don't be scared of any spirits who may try to frighten you by predicting death or disaster. A true guardian would never reveal such matters, and anyway, fate is not fixed. When you are working with friends, there is no reason for you to be asking questions about death or negative things, or speculating about them before a session.

Do not get involved with lost or troubled spirits or try to send them on their way. This is a skilled art and hazardous, even for a long-standing medium or healer. Certainly don't try to exorcise a house where there is negative paranormal activity – leave that to the priest or professional healer.

Do not start testing guides or demanding proof. Even a darker entity can read your mind or probe around your aura and so appear to know a lot about you. Equally, he or she can arrange a parking space or for a small cheque to arrive but that is not proof of good intention. It is better to establish a relationship that is undemanding with your main spirit or angel until you have built up the relationship or, if you already know them, to ask them to help you to contact other guides.

Remember a true guide will never tell you what to do or suggest an action that is morally dubious, nor try to turn you against people or feed you information that causes you to doubt friends or family. Your spirit guide is not likely to appear in a séance or through a ouija board and would never do anything to scare you or make you uneasy.

Don't become obsessed with talking to guides and spirits, even benign ones. If you are spending more time in spiritual realms than on your earthly interests, take time out to do gardening or physical exercise to restore the balance.

Don't work, even with your known guides, if you feel negative or angry. Meditate instead or occupy your mind with a mental task such as doing your accounting, transferring computer files or dealing with routine paperwork.

If you do encounter a spirit who makes you feel at all uneasy, then simply stop the communication. Sprinkle a clockwise circle of salt or drops of sacred water you have made (see page 227) around yourself and say: 'Go in peace'. If you have used any candles for the session, leave them burning in a safe place and have a bath or shower with any fragrant bath salts to restore your calm and protection.

The doorkeeper guardian

As you work with spirit guides and angels of all kinds, you may become aware of a shadow or slight shimmering, usually close to the physical door of the room or, if you are outdoors, near to a sheltering tree or large bush or rock. This is your doorkeeper guardian.

He or she acts as a gatekeeper against anything harmful from the spirit world approaching you as you talk to your guides. Later, when you are channelling wisdom from a higher being or if you decide to act as a mediator to help others to contact their relatives who are no longer with them, your doorkeeper becomes even more important.

There are ways to encourage your doorkeeper to give you psychic protection.

When you gain experience in spirit work, you will begin to develop your own protective radar that will ensure you are in contact only with benevolent spirits and alert you in the unlikely event that you encounter potential problems. However, your doorkeeper will always stand in the background, strengthening whatever methods of protection you use.

The first thing you can do is to set a protective doorkeeper crystal just inside the room in which you are working, so you can see it whether the door is open or closed. If you are working outside, place it near the tree or bush in the garden that forms an entrance to your working space. You do not have to use a crystal to activate your doorkeeper but it is a useful device.

You can look into the crystal before you begin and ask that your own doorkeeper will bless and protect you. Afterwards, wash the crystal under running water and keep it in white cloth until the next time you communicate with your spirit guides.

Doorkeeper crystals

The following are good doorkeeper crystals. You need only buy a very small one.

Phantom quartz: This is clear quartz crystal in which a phantom crystal appears. Phantom quartz occurs when the growth of the crystal is interrupted, and it leaves a shadowy, smaller crystal like a veil within the larger, host crystal. Sometimes another coloured crystal can grow around it, for example rose quartz or green chlorite. There are also green chlorite and rose quartz phantoms where clear quartz has grown around the coloured phantom (see page 55). Often the phantom quartz is in a pyramid shape.

Laser crystal: A channelling or laser crystal is a clear quartz crystal with seven edges surrounding the large, sloping face.

Isis crystal: This is named after the Ancient Egyptian mother goddess and is also clear quartz with five edges surrounding the largest sloping face.

Crystal sphere or pyramid: You can also use any crystal pyramid or small crystal sphere.

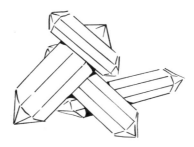

Protective crystals, herbs and oils

There are many protective crystals that you can use in spirit-guide work, and you can use whichever you feel attracted to. You only need small crystals. All these will be available in new-age stores.

Protective crystals: Black agate, amber, amethyst, bloodstone, carnelian, garnet, black and red jasper, jet, lapis lazuli, obsidian, rutilated quartz, smoky quartz, tiger's eye, topaz and turquoise.

Protective herbs, incenses and oils: Anise, basil, bay, carnation, cedarwood, cypress, frankincense, lavender, lemon, lemongrass, myrrh, nettle, peppermint, pine, rose, rosemary, sage, sandalwood, thyme and vanilla.

Ritual for angelic protection

If you are new to spirit work or to a particular aspect of it, angelic protection is a powerful but gentle way to encounter spirit guides in a protective atmosphere. This ritual is calming and relaxing and is a good way to start out with spirit-guide work.

You can set up your doorkeeper crystal at the beginning and wash it at the end of the spirit communication.

❏ Light four white candles, one half-way along each of the four walls of the room to mark the directions of north, south, east and west, using approximate directions from places you know. You can set each candle on small tables around the room or on the four sides of a table if you are working on one in the middle of the room.

❏ These candles represent the four archangels traditionally invoked for protection. They are Uriel, Archangel of the North and of Transformation, Raphael, the healing archangel in the East, Michael, Archangel of the Sun in the South and Gabriel, the Messenger Archangel of the Moon in the West.

❏ Light the candles clockwise from the east and name each archangel, asking for their protection. You can then begin to talk to your spirit guides.

❏ Afterwards, blow out the candles anti-clockwise from the north for continuing protection, thanking each guardian angel for blessings received.

Preparations for meeting your spirit guide

Especially when you are beginning in spirit-guide work, these techniques offer a good way to establish the right atmosphere in which to communicate with your spirit guides. They are also useful when you begin contact with those who are no longer with us or start exploring other dimensions when you go out into the wider spirit world. Follow the sequence set down until you become comfortable with it. You may then want to personalise it and develop your own ritual.

Before you begin spirit-guide work, make sure you have a quiet place to work. To start with, it can be any quiet spot, but if you are going to develop your spirit-guide work you may want to have a dedicated place, and I will talk more about that on page 28.

During the day before the session, eat and drink mainly uncooked or unprocessed pure food, then do not eat for an hour before a session.

❏ When you are ready, have a bath with relaxing rose or lavender essential oils or foam.

❏ Before you begin, make a small bowl of sacred water by adding three pinches of salt to a bowl of still mineral water, stirring the salt in clockwise with a silver knife. Then make the sign of the cross on the surface of the water.

❏ Place your sacred water on the table or outdoors where you are working. Place dishes of salt or cloves of garlic or a small dish of protective herbs (see page 21) on any window ledges in the room you are working in, or in pots on the ground if working outdoors, to exclude all external negative influences. Also keep a tiny dish of salt on the table.

❏ Place one or two small protective crystals (see page 21) around yourself.

❏ Play some soft, gently flowing music as a background to attract your guides. Bad spirits hate harmonious sounds.

❏ Burn some oil or incense in a protective fragrance (see pages 16–17) to attract your guides but also to deter any who would harm you. You can also use pot-pourri or fresh or dried petals in the room or sit near fragrant flowers outdoors.

❏ Activate your doorkeeper.

❏ Begin spirit contact by establishing a light source. You can rely on natural light; sunlight during the day or bright moonlight after dark. If the day is dark or you are working in the evening on a moonless night, light a white or beeswax candle near where you will be working. Alternatively, use a fibre optic lamp (the traditional red light used for spirit communication is a bit spooky). Darker spirits do not like light.

You can then proceed with contacting your spirit guides, and I outline below what to expect.

Your first spiritual encounter

If you are meeting spirit guides for the first time, the first and probably only one you will encounter will be your special guide. Even if you have worked with spirit guides before, the following method is a good way of learning more about your special guide. Do not be surprised, however, if you see a different guide as well if you are experienced, perhaps one who is just moving into your life for a specific purpose.

The following technique is centred round the sensory channels your spirit guide loves most: sound, light and fragrance.

❑ Activate your doorkeeper.

❑ Hang a tiny wind chime over where you will be working (unless you ring a bell as in the following archangel invocation).

❑ Light a pure white or beeswax candle in front of you.

❑ Set an incense stick in a flat holder on either side of the candle, so the sticks are at a 60° angle. Frankincense, myrrh or sandalwood are ceremonial fragrances to create contact with other dimensions and are also very protective.

❑ Light each stick from the candle and return it to its holder, so the smoke from each curls above the candle flame. If necessary, slightly open a window so the flame and smoke move continuously.

❑ With half-closed eyes, gaze into the moving area around the candle flame and the smoke and allow a moving image to build up either around the flame and smoke or in your mind's vision.

❑ The key is to allow the picture to form, not to force it. If you are finding this difficult, close your eyes and let the picture start forming against the dark screen of your mind. Then open your eyes suddenly and gaze at the candle flame and the smoke.

❑ You may see only a face or have an impression of a figure rather than a three-dimensional picture. Your guide may not be at all what you expected, but as you get to know each other, you will understand the purpose of the connection.

❑ For now, speak softly and say you are glad to meet your guide and that you wish to learn more about him or her. In return you may hear words in your mind, either in your own voice or one that is clearer, deeper or just different. This will not be the key to the universe, but something you were wondering or worrying about, and perhaps a little about your guide.

❑ You can ask now the name of the guide. Accept whatever name you are given without question. It may be the name the guide used during his or her last incarnation on Earth or a special spiritual name he or she chose. What is more, even if your guide is called, for example, Michael, don't assume you have the archangel himself in your presence, as there are lots of Michaels. Your guide may have taken the archangel name as his spiritual one because he is very courageous or is surrounded by light. You may find references to the name if you check later in mythological or spiritual source books but, if you do not, it does not mean the name is not valid.

❑ Your guide may appear surrounded by coloured lights (more of this on page 32) or may seem quite hazy. You may glimpse a setting through the light – a garden, a temple or monastery, an old stone circle, a forest or a cave – that may tell you a little about your guide.

Each time you work, these pictures will get clearer, and one day you will be able to visit the guide in his or her natural setting (see page 133).

While your personal guide may be a Native North American medicine man, a Viking wise woman or an Ancient Egyptian priest or priestess, these more elevated guardians are usually teachers who appear at times when we need wisdom (see page 56). Your main guide may be less easy to identify at this stage, so be patient.

The first session is usually brief, and when you feel the energies fading, let the experience likewise fade. At this point, even if your guide is no longer visible, thank him or her and establish a signal for making contact when you are not able to sit with a candle and incense or one of the other, more formal methods described in the book.

For example, you could choose touching the centre of your brow (the location of the third, or psychic clairvoyant, eye), clasping your hands together or, if you know the guide's name, calling it three times softly, aloud or in your mind.

❑ Finally, blow out the candle and send the light to whoever needs it, including yourself. Leave the incense to burn through.

❑ Sit quietly for a while, as the experience will be tiring, then ground your energies (see below).

❑ Thank your doorkeeper and wash his or her crystal.

❑ Afterwards, have a drink and perhaps some light food and note down any features you noticed, sensations you experienced and any message you received.

❑ You can start a special book of spirit communication (see page 29) so that you have notes of your experiences with your spirit guides.

You may see your guide in a dream the same night.

Grounding yourself

After any spirit communication, you should thank your doorkeeper and wash his or her crystal, if you used one. Then it is important to ground yourself, otherwise your mind and body will be buzzing all night and you will not be properly psychically closed down. Sit or stand quietly and press down with your hands on the table and your feet on the floor to drain away any excess energy. Outdoors you can press barefoot into the ground and hold your hands by your sides, fingers together and pointing down.

You can then clear up and write down your experiences in your journal (see page 29).

The archangel invocation

For special occasions when you work with your spirit guides, use this archangel invocation. It is good if you have had troublesome dreams or for any reason feel afraid or anxious. This time leave the four archangel candles unlit. I suggest using yellow, gold, silver and red candles but you can use just four white ones.

❑ Ring a silver bell in each of the four main directions in front of the candles.

❑ Then say:

> *I invite my loved ones who are with me no more, my wise guides, my guardian angel and the beings of light to enter this room and to communicate if it is right to be.*

You can leave out mention of loved ones if it worries you.

❑ First, face east, the direction of dawn, the rising sun and of spring.

❑ Light a yellow candle, calling upon the healing energies of Raphael, saying:

> *Gentle Raphael with your healing staff, protect me from spectres of the night, troubled spirits and all who come with dark intent. May there be only light here and purity and may I and those who work with me from other realms be guided only by goodness and pure intention.*

❑ Face south, direction of the noonday sun and summer.

❑ Light a gold candle, calling upon the light-bringing powers of Michael, saying:

> *Mighty Michael with your golden sword, protect me from spectres of the night, troubled spirits and all who come with dark intent. May there be only light here and purity and may I and those who work with me from other realms be guided only by goodness and pure intention.*

❑ Face the west, the direction of sunset and autumn.

❑ Light a silver candle, calling upon the wise counsel of Gabriel, the messenger, saying:

> *Wise Gabriel, guide of all who follow the spiritual path, protect me from spectres of the night, troubled spirits and all who come with dark intent. May there be only light here and purity and may I and those who work with me from other realms be guided only by goodness and pure intention.*

❑ Finally, face north and light a red candle, calling upon the transforming and cleansing powers of Uriel, saying:

> *Great Uriel, archangel of change and cleansing fire, protect me from spectres of the night, troubled spirits and all who come with dark intent. May there be only light here and purity and may I and those who work with me from other realms be guided only by goodness and pure intention.*

❐ Now light your special pure white or beeswax candle and talk to your permanent guide or another guardian (see pages 23–5 and 31–3).

❐ When you have finished talking to your guide/s, blow out the candle you used with your guide and then the archangel candles in reverse order, thanking each archangel for protection and blessings.

❐ Ring your bell again at the four directions in reverse order: north, west, south and east.

❐ Then say:

> *I thank my loved ones who are with me no more, my wise guides, angels and beings of light who have guided and protected me. Let us part in peace until we meet again.*

Again omit loved ones if you prefer.

Creating a special place for spirit communication

While you can encounter and communicate with your spirit guides in any place at any time, try to find a room or outbuilding in your home where you can work with your spirit guides and angels for longer periods and will not be disturbed or distracted. This area need not be large and could even be part of your bedroom that you curtain off.

Here you can keep a fresh white candle on a table covered with a dark cloth, ready for your work, with some incense or incense sticks in protective and empowering fragrances, one or two of your favourite protective crystals (see pages 138–44 for suggestions) on the table, and a larger crystal sphere or pyramid you will use for more advanced work.

Also on the table have a vase of fresh flowers that you replace regularly, or a pot of protective herbs (see pages 145–9 for suggestions).

Have a comfortable chair or, if you prefer sitting on the ground, use a low table and cushions.

The room can be left prepared with lidded dishes of salt, a covered bowl of water and a silver knife ready to make your sacred water immediately before the contact. You could have a special display place for your doorkeeper crystal and tables ready around the walls with fresh candles should you wish to call on the archangels.

After meditation or spirit contact, once you have grounded yourself, clear away the materials from the old ritual and prepare fresh ones ready for future work.

You can also keep in a drawer in the room any divination tools you use, such as Tarot, runes, small crystals, or a crystal pendulum so that you can ask your guides to use these to give you answers.

Have also white paper and a black pen and ink for when you try channelling wisdom through automatic writing (see page 59). The pen should be used only for this purpose.

Make sure you have staples such as matches and envelopes for spirit letters (see page 40) so that you are ready at any time you are able to spend even a few minutes drawing wisdom and strength.

Finally, choose a plain-leafed book to use as a journal in which you can write your spirit communications and rituals. It need not be elaborate, but again you should keep a special pen. You can also use this book to write the names of people you know who need healing when you work with healing guides or angels (see pages 34 and 120).

You can work outdoors as well and may be able to find a sheltered place in your garden with a flat surface (or use a picnic table) where you can lay out your main tools for spirit work. Outdoors you could plant four small bushes around where you work or have small trees in tubs to act as your guardian archangel foci and perhaps use solar lighting or outdoor lights behind them after dark.

3

Getting to know your spirit guides

A s you get to know your personal spirit guide better, you will become aware of when he or she has moved into your personal energy space and is ready to communicate with you. This is akin to sitting with your back to the door and being aware that someone has come into the room even though they may be moving silently on thick carpet or standing on the threshold. You may also already get a buzzing in your head a minute or so before a friend or family member telephones or is coming up the path, even if the contact is not at a usual time. This buzzing is a similar sensation to that associated with the presence of a spirit guide, but is softer and more subtle.

In this chapter we will explore various ways of communicating with your guide and with other guardians to whom he or she may introduce you who can help you in your life.

Becoming aware of the signals

As with earthly communication, there is usually a good reason for an unexpected visit by your spirit guide. Your spirit guide will have anticipated when you need to speak to him or her, even if you do not realise it yourself on a conscious level. In time you will literally feel your special guide, and other wise teachers and healers, moving close as a slight pressure as though someone is gently pressing the top of your head or a cobweb brushing against your face, even in an open place.

Your fingers may start tingling. Colours will suddenly seem brighter, sounds more acute and fragrances stronger as your psychic senses temporarily take over from your physical ones. In fact what is happening is your spirit guide raising your spiritual energy vibrations or level of awareness. At the same time he or she lowers and slows down their own spiritual rate so you can communicate clearly with them, even if you are quite new to spiritual work (see more on this in Chapter 4).

Spirit guides don't have human bodies as such because they are pure spirit form, vibrating faster than the speed of light and so don't need a body (see Chapter 5 for more on this). However, when they appear, they will often assume the form they took in their last life.

At first you may find you see your guide mainly through a coloured mist or as flashes and sparks of light, and may notice one of more orbs of light (called spirit orbs) on photographs of yourself, which show your guardians are with you. But you can hear them telepathically within your mind, and sometimes they will send a message by moving objects or telling you to switch on the radio while driving or to look at a particular road sign, whose significance may later become clear.

Communication is like tuning in to a hard-to-find satellite-television station and gradually not only the words but also the pictures get clearer. As you talk over months and years to your spirit guide, you will be developing your clairvoyant (psychic, or inner-eye vision) and clairaudient (or inner psychic ear hearing) powers. These are quite normal extensions of the physical senses and as you work with spirit energies these innate powers will spontaneously emerge.

Places and times for spirit communication

Over the months, too, you will discover certain places and times, as well as the special sanctuary you created in the previous chapter, where your spirit guide communicates most clearly with you. Is it during an evening walk with the dog, on a Sunday morning, in the garden, on a windy day in the woods or sitting at your office desk at night when the building is quiet?

Just before you go to sleep and as you wake are good times for spirit contact because your conscious mind is relaxed and so you can more easily receive impressions from other dimensions.

Meditation is also good for creating this altered sense of awareness (see page 57 in the next chapter).

The nature of communication may change according to the need and as the relationship develops – and indeed as you encounter other guides. In this chapter and the following chapters I have suggested a number of methods to enrich these special times and prepare you for the later stages of spirit communication if you wish to develop further.

Some people are happy to communicate only with their spirit guide and guardian angel, but others wish to learn from teachers and healers from other dimensions or to explore the astral or spirit planes. Be patient and when you are spiritually ready (perhaps sooner or later than you would have anticipated) your guide will allow you access to higher realms.

Other spirit guides you may meet

But first, let's consider other spirit guides you may meet as you come to know your personal guardian better. They were also once human and exist at a similar level of spirit to your main guardian. Because of this they are accessible to you even in the early stages of your exploration. I have written about your ever-present guardian angel on page 49 onwards.

Helper spirits

These guides can teach and guide us in different aspects of our daily lives and help us to learn new skills. Later you may meet the master teachers and more elevated spiritual guides who may increase your own higher knowledge and healing powers (see page 57). But helper guides will teach you skills you need right now in your present life and so are very important; for example, if you are a schoolteacher, you will have a guardian schoolteacher helping you. As you learn new skills, perhaps healing or alternative medicine, or start to write your first novel, so a guide who has served their apprenticeship in the same skill on Earth (though not necessarily one whose name is familar to you) can ease your path. You may eventually learn their name and if you persevere and remain eager to learn, they might eventually take you along to a masterclass with one of the big players.

Linda, a nurse, had worked since childhood with her spirit guide, Margaret, who had once lived in a religious community taking care of the garden and making medicines from the herbs. Margaret was the perfect complement to Linda's fast pace of life, trying to achieve everything in five minutes. She had taught Linda to look at the world around and to think before speaking or acting.

When Linda was accepted to nurse sick children in Africa, Margaret started to bring along a tall, beautiful African woman who at first said little. But as Linda struggled to learn the language of the area she was moving to, she became aware of a slow, melodic voice in her mind, helping her to pronounce the words.

When Linda was first in Africa and her newly acquired vocabulary failed, suddenly the correct word would come into her mind, spoken in the same rich voice, and Linda realised that her African spirit guide was with her. Though Linda never knew her new guide's name, she had a vivid image of the woman: tall, stately and with a white-pigmented heart shape on her face. In the locality were legends of a tall, wise grandmother called 'the Heart Woman' because of a facial feature. The Heart Woman had assisted the first missionaries to bring medical aid to her people.

When Linda returned to the UK her African guide left her.

If you need particular help with a skill, ask your personal guide to introduce you to another guide who will help you to learn. The only requirement is that you do work hard at the new skill and do not expect the new guide to do it all, or expect a great poet or musician to help you before you have mastered the basics.

Your spirit physician

If you feel exhausted or constantly unwell for a period and conventional or alternative healing is not helping, you can ask your spirit guide for the advice and help of a spirit physician. Spirit physicians are doctors and healers from a variety of traditions who were once human healers. Your spirit guide will introduce you to whoever will best help. Often a spirit physician will come during sleep and will bring healing in a dream or suggest healing remedies. Along with the remedy you may recall only the voice or face of your healer. This is very different from learning healing yourself from wise guides, and I have written more about this in the section on healing.

For example, David is a sales manager and has suffered for years from skin problems that medicine has not helped. Though David has never talked to his spirit guide, he has often dreamed of an old priest who is always very kind to him. Recently, the priest (obviously David's personal spirit guide) was accompanied into David's dreams by a person who was by dress and appearance an Ancient Egyptian priest. The Ancient Egyptian told David in the dream he had once worked at the temple of Denderah. This temple was sacred to the Egyptian goddess Hathor, and here the Egyptian priest made healing medicines. The Ancient Egyptian informed David that he should add rose essential oil to his morning bath and use a rose healing cream.

David woke to the scent of roses though he never had flowers in his apartment. Curious but sceptical, the logical David went into a pharmacy and bought some rose essential oil and cream. Within a few weeks of using them his skin problems greatly improved.

Even stranger, while David was away on business, an evening appointment was cancelled and he turned on the television in his hotel room. On the screen was the temple of Denderah (of which David had never heard before the dream). The presenter said it was sacred to the Egyptian mother goddess Hathor and here priests created secret perfumes and oils for healing.

Methods of working with guides

Floating candles

This follows on naturally from the candle exercise in the previous chapter. If you found your guardian spirit remained elusive in the candle flame, this method stimulates the inner, or clairvoyant, eye into giving clear form to the presence you sensed. It also brings the image of your guide into close focus so you can follow on from your earlier candle work.

Because the candles are constantly moving, creating light patterns on the water, you can more easily see a face in the water, perhaps more than one if helper guides are present.

❑ After dark, light a frankincense or myrrh incense stick behind a glass bowl of water. If your guardian has a special accompanying fragrance, light incense or oil in that fragrance instead.

❑ Float three or four silver or gold candles on the surface of the water.

❑ Light them one by one.

❑ Once the candles are alight, extinguish any other light and draw curtains if there is a street lamp outside.

❑ Look into the surface of the water slightly from the side so your own reflection is not within the water.

❑ Gently push the candles so they move faster over the surface creating changing patterns of light on the water. The idea is to trick your conscious eye into allowing your clairvoyant eye to see your guide reflected in the water.

❑ Call your guide with the special signal you established in the earlier candle ritual, such as calling his or her name three times softly or touching your brow, and say:

> I welcome you in love and light and ask that you may
> make your presence known to me.

There may be a slight breeze even if the window is shut.

❑ Focus on the dark water between the light pools and you may first see a slight shimmer, then a shadowy outline of the face of your guide.

❑ Or you may see the face entirely in your mind, which is just as good.

❑ Relax and allow the figure to build downwards (either in your mind or on the water surface) from the face and the details to become clearer, as though putting a camera in focus.

How to talk with your guide

❑ Even if the figure is hazy, speak softly and ask your guide to tell you who he or she is, when you were first guided and a little about the guide's former life on Earth. The information you seek will vary according to how much you gained from the earlier candle ritual. You could ask if he or she is known by any other names and whether that is their Earth name or has been chosen for a particular reason.

❑ Pause between questions and listen for a reply in your mind. The difference between imagination and the words of a guide is that there is a slight bumping sensation in your mind like a car changing gear when the guide speaks. Your fingers may tingle and you may become aware of sparks of light or colours around the room or in the water.

❑ Continue to look at the water and your guide may show you symbols, pictures that hold the key to questions you have not yet asked.

They will be symbols that mean something to you personally, but you may mainly pick up impressions from the spirit encounter which do not come in words or even images, but through another power we all possess called 'clairsentience', or clear sensing.

In this way you know about your guide without being specifically told and understand without words the path that brought you to this time and place together.

Ask your guide about anything that is troubling or challenging you, about yourself, family or friends. Talk about your secret dreams and needs. You don't need to plan the dialogue, but let it develop in its own way.

Communication with your personal guide tends not, as I said earlier, to be about the nature of the universe, but to focus on personal issues you may not even feel able to share with your partner, your mother or your best friend.

❑ Just talk and listen and keep moving the candles so that the patterns of the water and light allow your higher sense of awareness to take control. You may talk for two, five or ten minutes or half an hour or until the candles go out.

❑ Ask your guide if he or she has any special message for you.

❑ Before you end your contact, enquire if there are any other guardians who might be willing to talk to you or help you in the immediate future and if you might see them in the water.

❑ Close your eyes and look once more into the dark water between the candles. You may see a helper guide or a wise physician or healer, or there may be no other guide if this is not the right time. But almost always you will sense another wise presence. They will not speak now, but may come to you when you are asleep or while you are occupied in the task with which the helper will guide you – and because they were introduced by your guide you know they are true helpers.

☐ Thank your guide/s and end with your special sign to the guide and sit quietly looking into the water until the candles go out.

☐ Light another candle or a small lamp and write about your experience in your spirit journal. Let a story naturally unfold about your special guide and you may become aware that he or she is dictating the words.

How to meet your spirit guide in a dream

Some people first encounter their spirit guide in dreams. This may be a wise figure that appears in a number of dreams, talking to us reassuringly, offering unconditional support and friendship. Answers and inspiration may come through such dreams and when we wake the dream remains vivid, colourful and immensely comforting, though we may regret we could not stay longer in the beautiful setting where such dreams often take place.

Because in sleep our unconscious mind is in control, spirit guides can talk to us without the conscious barriers.

Once you have identified your spirit guides through one of the candle methods (or the crystal sphere technique described on pages 50–1), you can use your dreams creatively to work with them and with your helper guides. You can also open yourself to receiving healing, whether regular top-ups of energy or for specific conditions from your physician guide, who operates mainly during sleep.

The following techniques are adapted from the rituals practised by the Ancient Egyptians, Greeks and Romans in their healing dream temples, where individuals went to receive guidance and help in the dream state. You can read more about the powers of dreams and of dream symbols in my dream book, *Cassandra Eason's Modern Book of Dream Interpretation*, (Foulsham/Quantum, 2005).

Dream work will form an important part of other chapters of the book, but for now I will concentrate on the basic building blocks of dream work. Even if you already work with dreams, you may find this alternative route a fast entry point to dream work.

Dream communication

The first thing you will need is a notebook and pen or another way of recording the details of your spirit encounters as soon as you wake, before details fade. A hand-held dictating machine would be ideal.

You will also need a special sleep crystal, not to see your guide in but to hold as a channel and protection for night work to establish the link between you and those guides who will visit you in sleep.

Good sleep-channelling crystals: These include rose quartz, amethyst, any fluorite or tourmaline, aqua or cobalt aura or a glistening opal aura crystal that is filled with rainbows. Effective also is a blue goldstone, which looks like the night sky filled with stars, a stone related to the alchemist's stone of old which was believed to turn base metals into gold. It need only be small and should be kept in a blue or purple pouch or purse in a drawer by your bed when not in use.

Even if this method does not seem to work for a while, keep trying, as once you have learned to create a protected meeting place on the dream plane you can at a later date use it as a safe base from which to explore higher realms. Much later you will be able to realise when you are dreaming (a technique called 'lucid', or clear, dreaming) and so are in no physical danger. Then you can work with your guides in all kinds of exciting ways.

But back to the beginning:

- ❑ Switch off phones and faxes, and try to make a time before sleep when you can be alone and undisturbed.

- ❑ Have a light supper and avoid stimulating television programmes, instead spending the evening listening to gentle music.

- ❑ Before sleep, place small scented candles around the bathroom and relax in a bath to which a little rose or lavender oil has been added.

- ❑ After your bath, carry one or two of the candles into the bedroom and, sitting up in bed, hold your sleep crystal in your cupped hands.

- ❑ Recite any question or request for knowledge or healing you may have seven times.

- ❑ Still holding the crystal, close your eyes and picture your guide or a helper or healer (perhaps your guide with the helper) walking towards you.

- ❑ Say:

> Come to me in my dreams. I carry my crystal into sleep
> and within it I will hear your message.

❏   Blow out the candles and place your crystal next to your bed.

❏   Lie with your eyes closed and repeat the words softly until they fade, picturing your crystal becoming larger until you are within it, safe and enclosed. Your crystal may take the shape of a tall crystal pyramid, a crystal temple or a crystal cave.

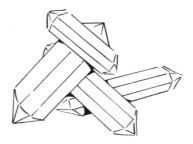

At first you may dream of your guides spontaneously or see pictures and scenes that hold the answers. Accept this and be patient, for each dream involving your guides or answers to questions you asked before sleep is an important part of the process of working creatively with guides on the dream plane.

If you persevere with the crystal dream technique (twice a week is enough, as you need spontaneous dreams as well), within a few weeks you will be creating or, as the Greeks called it, 'incubating' your dream. In this way you do see the crystal place in dreams and can work within this protected place on the dream plane.

Once this happens you can meet within the crystal structure the guide who can best answer your question or your spirit physician – perhaps more than one guide will be waiting. Here you will learn the answers you seek, and may be helped by a teacher guide with a skill you are finding hard to learn.

Afterwards, even if you have not asked pre-sleep a question about your health, your wise doctor guide may come to make sure you are well, perhaps giving you healing for a problem of which you are not yet consciously aware, and offering necessary, if not always welcome, advice about keeping yourself healthy. You may be given the information as symbols or images, which means you will have to work harder to interpret your answers in the morning.

Your guides may take you beyond the pyramid to show you healing remedies or perhaps take you to a workshop or school where you will learn a particular lesson or craft. When this has ended you will find yourself within the crystal formation again, the scene will fade and you will wake gently.

- ❏ Hold your crystal in one hand as soon as you wake, and write down everything you can recall. Do not try to return to the dream place, even if you were woken suddenly by household sounds. Nor should you try to analyse the dream.

- ❏ Relax and drift back into sleep.

- ❏ When you wake in the morning, or after you have recorded the information if you slept all night, allow the ideas to flow through your mind.

- ❏ Wash your dream crystal, allow it to dry naturally, preferably in natural light, and return it to the pouch.

During the day the dream work should start to make sense.

If it doesn't, use the images and feelings the dream invoked to weave a story in which you take the starring role and that will put the information into context.

Spirit-guide dream letters

Dream letters come from the Ancient Egyptian tradition and were used to gain help and advice from the deities and from ancestors dwelling in the afterlife. Sometimes these were not letters as we would think of them at all, but words written round the edges of a pottery bowl in which offerings such as fruit or flowers were left as tribute. However, there were almost certainly more conventional letters, created on linen or papyrus, spoken aloud and then burned in a lamp or candle.

Writing a letter containing requests for healing or answers to questions is a good way of making clear in your own mind what it is you need. Your spirit guide and helpers are very amenable to any form of communication and will bring you answers to your questions both in spontaneous dreams and by symbols or signals during the following day; for example you may suddenly hear a tune whose title answers your question.

The idea of writing also leads on to the skill of automatic writing to communicate with higher guides and ancestors. We will work with this on page 59.

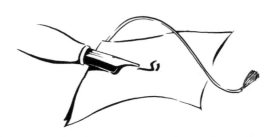

Keep a special pad of white paper, a black pen and an envelope next to your bed (not the same paper you use for recording dreams).

❑ Before sleep, sit up in bed and, by the light of a small lamp, write what it is you want to know or the way you or a family member or friend needs healing. Write also anything you are having trouble learning or succeeding in. Do not worry if it all comes out in a jumble or by the end of the letter you are altering what you asked for originally. Spirit guides are remarkably good at understanding what we are really saying and thinking.

❑ You can, if you wish, begin by naming your special guide or with 'Dear Wise Physician' or just go straight into the letter. If you wish, divide the material into three letters, one for questions for your guide, one for the physician and one for your teacher if you are working with all three.

❑ End with thanks and sign your name. Put the letter or letters into the same envelope and seal it.

❑ On the front, draw the protective Egyptian hieroglyph (pictorial sign) shown here for the Ka, the part of the soul that guarded the Egyptian mummy and which is also associated with protection during sleep. The Ka was represented by the hieroglyph of two outstretched arms.

❑ Place the envelope, symbol upwards, beneath your pillow.

❑ Leave it there for seven nights, by which time answers or healing should have come to you in your dreams or as symbols in your everyday world.

❑ Destroy the letter after this time as its work is done.

Try to do something positive for others or the environment as a way of expressing thanks.

Using a crystal pendulum to communicate with your spirit guide

This is probably the easiest way to communicate with your personal spirit guide and you can also use this method of questioning if you have a teacher guide who is assisting you in a venture. Spirit physicians tend to be very busy, but will usually answer questions no more than once a week using the pendulum.

If the methods I have suggested earlier for spirit communication are not proving fruitful, adopt the pendulum method and then retry the others. Any blockages in communication will have cleared.

The pendulum is operated by the involuntary muscle movement in your arm. This movement is normally controlled by your intuitive mind, which can receive information from sources not bound by measured time. For example, if at 1pm in London you were phoning a friend in, say, Stockholm, he or she would be in your future, as it would be 2pm for them. If you were contacting someone in Los Angeles it would be only 5am their time. So even measured time is only relative and your spirit guide would refer only to your time to avoid waking you in the middle of the night.

When you use the pendulum to channel information from your spirit guides, you are not being taken over or possessed by them. Rather, you are allowing the guide who is communicating to move the pendulum using your muscles, just as you allow the words of your spirit guide to be heard through your inner voice and ear. It is no different from someone putting their hands over yours while you use a tool for the first time. Any time you want to stop, you can put the pendulum down and break the link.

A clear quartz crystal pendulum is probably best for spirit-guide work. It need not be a large one, but keep it just for this kind of work and not for more general dowsing.

Beginning pendulum communication

If you have not used a pendulum before, first you need to establish your Yes/No, Act/Wait, Speak/Listen response.

To discover the positive (Yes/Act/Speak) response, think of a time when you were really happy and everything went right. The pendulum will usually swing in a clockwise circle, but you should go with the response you get. Your spirit guide/s will use that response.

Now think of a sad time or one when things went wrong. Your pendulum will give its negative (No/Wait/Listen) response, which will often be the reverse of the positive one, for example an anti-clockwise circle, though it may be something quite different.

Finally, you need to discover your 'Ask again' response. Your pendulum, even if controlled by the Archangel Gabriel, can only answer 'Yes' or 'No' and not respond to an either/or choice. So if you said to your guide: 'Will I feel more settled by spring?' the answer would be 'Yes' or 'No', but if you asked: 'Will I be settled by the spring or must I wait till summer?' your pendulum could not give a direct reply. Therefore the pendulum would make its 'Ask again' movement. It might also make this if what you asked infringed the privacy of another person or was not answerable right now because of factors that were yet to come into play.

Think of a time when you got lost or were confused, and your pendulum will make its 'Ask again' response, often by randomly swinging clockwise and anti-clockwise.

❐ Use one of the psychic protection methods listed in the previous chapter so that you deter any mischievous or time-wasting spirits.

❐ Sit in your special place or somewhere where the pendulum will not be blown by the wind.

❐ First you need to cleanse your pendulum so that you will attract only your own guides or those who will be helpful to you.

❐ Fortunately, clear quartz crystal deters all but spirits of light. However, as a precaution, use a large glass bowl half-filled with sparkling mineral water and plunge your pendulum rapidly into it nine times, saying:

> *May only purity and goodness be transmitted though*
> *this pendulum. Blessings be.*

❐ Alternatively, light a miniature sage or cedar smudge or incense stick and make alternate anti-clockwise and clockwise spirals of smoke round the pendulum, using the same blessing.

❑ When it is cleansed, wait until you can detect your guide's fragrance or presence. Then make your special signal, for example calling your guide's name three times softly, and ask if he or she will speak through the pendulum.

❑ If the answer is 'No', ask whether another guide wishes to speak to you instead.

❑ If 'Yes', you can ask questions to discover the identity of the guide, who may be your current teacher or physician. Your personal guide will know if you need special help and will just have come along to make sure only the approved guide is allowed to talk to you.

❑ However, if at any time you feel uneasy and that the guide you are talking to is changing into someone you do not know or the answers are becoming unhelpful (unlikely with all this protection), put down the pendulum, say: 'Go in peace' and cleanse the pendulum using one of the above methods.

Crossed wires occur even on celestial planes. A genuine guide will never mind and will return to reassure you later if you just got nervous without reason.

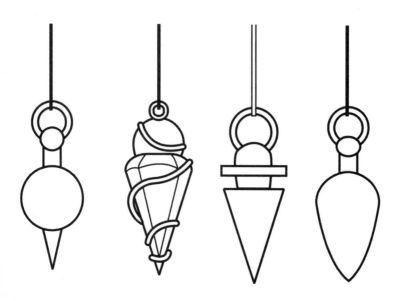

Asking the right questions

❐ Hold your pendulum in your power hand; the one you write with.

❐ Formulate your first direct question according to the guide to whom you are talking. You may wish to speak it aloud. Take your time in asking and be patient if the pendulum responds slowly.

❐ Put down the pendulum and scribble down the question and response.

❐ Then, holding the pendulum again, allow the next question to come into your mind. This may not be at all what you expected, especially if the previous answer was: 'Ask again'. After each response, scribble down the question and answer.

❐ Continue until you feel the energies ebbing and then thank your guide and say: 'Until we meet again', followed by your personal signal.

❐ If you have been talking to a teacher or your physician guide, thank this guide first and then your personal guide, who facilitated the meeting.

❐ Cleanse the pendulum again, this time in silence.

Read through the questions and answers and you will see how your guide/s, like any good teacher, actually led you to discover the necessary information yourself, whether it was advice on altering your diet or about the reliability of a new earthly friend of whom you may be uncertain. The greatest gift our guides can give us is to help us use our own innate and higher wisdom. The more you work with your guides the more self-reliant you become.

4

Working with angels and higher spirit guides

re guardian angels and spirit guides different? Some people would argue they are not. However, many people do recognise both an angel and a spirit guide who cares for them in their lives.

In this chapter I will write of angels specifically in their protective role as they are an important form of spiritual guardian and are also another step towards our understanding and experience of more elevated spiritual beings.

The differences between angels and spirit guides

I suppose the most obvious difference is that, unlike our spirit guides, angels never lived as humans, but are altogether a different kind of being.

Evidence through the ages and in a variety of cultures gives remarkably consistent descriptions of the external appearance of angels. This would indicate that these higher beings do have an existence independent of human thought. Even the more approachable guardian angel is made of pure energy that vibrates at a level we possess only in the outer, more spiritual layers of our aura, or personal energy field.

Your spirit guide is like a dear friend who has experienced and overcome human temptations and frailties, and so you can talk and ask about anything.

We work best initially with angels through very informal prayer, meditation or using a crystal sphere or ball (see pages 50–1). As you become more spiritually evolved through connection with higher dimensions, so direct angelic communication becomes easier.

Children have no difficulties; they see and talk to their angels as easily as they do other spirit beings, such as fairies and invisible friends. This is because children operate quite naturally on all spiritual levels before their auras get weighed down by earthly matters. Much spiritual work involves relearning those forgotten childhood powers, but as adults in ways in which we can control and direct our innate abilities.

Angels are associated with religion and appear in all the major world religions including Christianity, Judaism and Islam. Of course, we can talk to and receive help from angels even if we belong to no formal religion. However, they are traditionally viewed within the context of the belief in the existence of an ultimate divine force, even if such a concept is very hazy to us. Spirit guides primarily relate to us in a personal, non-specifically religious though always spiritual, capacity.

While our spirit guides can be male or female and have quite distinctive personalities, angels are androgynous and are beautiful and loving. They will always accept us as we are and love us, though they have not experienced negative thoughts or actions personally. Some people do experience their special angel as either specifically male or female and angels can modify their appearance to answer our particular need and thought frames.

Angelic experiences

While we may choose to acknowledge and work with our spirit guides or not, our guardian angel hovers around even when we are at our most difficult or unwilling to acknowledge our spiritual nature. Given the constraints of free will and the unknown cosmic factors that even angels abide by, our guardian angel generally ensures we are kept safe, sometimes from our own stupidity or a momentary lapse of attention at a crucial time.

Courtney, an art student who lives in Washington State in America, fell asleep at the wheel of his car. It crashed into a concrete bridge and turned over. Courtney woke on impact, upside-down and covered in glass, in darkness on a deserted country road. Suddenly an urgent voice told him to get out of the car, but Courtney could not find the seat-belt release. He panicked and felt a hand gently helping him to find and unfasten the release button. He tried to crawl across the crushed ceiling, but was unable to fight his way out of the car. As he cried out for help, he found himself floating outside the car, surrounded by a brilliant light, more dazzling than any he had ever seen. He closed his eyes because the light was so bright.

When he opened them, the radiance was gone. But the danger was not over. As he stood in the darkness, stunned, a voice told the teenager to run as fast as he could. Seconds later, the car burst into flames and was completely destroyed. So fierce had been the impact of the crash that the engine had gone through the floor. Courtney, however, escaped with minor cuts and bruises. The only spot where the car's ceiling was not completely crushed was the small area where Courtney's head had been. Like Courtney, those who saw the wreckage could offer no earthly explanation for his survival.

Angels, it is said, herald the moment of our birth and when we leave this world. For this reason some midwives have described to me a golden light surrounding mother and child at the birth. Other nurses in hospices have reported seeing a similar glow around the time of a patient dying, an experience that may be shared by relatives as well as the dying person.

Alice saw an angel next to her dying mother's bedside, tall and very beautiful, with silver-tipped, feathery wings and a wonderful circlet of silver on golden hair. It seemed the wings were enfolding her mother, who had been heavily sedated for some time. Suddenly her mother sat up and smiled and Alice said her mother's face became golden and looked for a moment young again, and unravaged by illness. 'Oh Alice,' she said, 'I saw the silver angel and his wings were soft, like a pillow. I am so happy.'

Shortly afterwards, Alice's mother died.

Contacting your guardian angel

You may already have sensed the presence of your special angel or seen him or her in dreams or meditation. You may even regularly contact your angelic presence. The following method incorporates prayer, which simply means talking aloud or in your mind to a higher power in a quiet, sacred setting. Your indoor or outdoor place where you encounter your spirit guide and teachers is an ideal spot to talk to your angel. However, you may discover a local ruined abbey, a corner in a church or cathedral (even if you do not attend services), or a beautiful garden where your angel always feels close.

If you have asked a question or for help or guidance, an angelic answer often comes later as either help in your life or sudden illumination or inspiration when you are quiet and relaxed.

Though we do have one special angel from birth to death, others may draw close at times when you need special help.

Try this method whether you work regularly with your angel or have never encountered him or her before. You can also use this when you sense a different angel around you who you feel has wisdom for you.

Stage 1

❑ Find your peaceful spot outdoors in soft sun or moonlight.

❑ If you would prefer to work indoors, light a beeswax-, lavender- or rose-scented candle for angel work.

❏ Sit comfortably. Close your eyes and breathe in very gently and slowly through your nose and out again so that one breath follows another in an unbroken stream.

❏ Picture a beautiful butterfly resting on each foot. Hold your feet as still as you can while you gently inhale and then, as the butterflies move upwards, relax and exhale.

❏ Next, see the butterflies on your knees and again as you inhale, hold your knees motionless so as not to disturb them.

❏ Exhale gently and slowly while they are in the air again.

❏ Continue as they land together on your navel, then separately on your hands, separately on each breast, together on the throat, separately on each shoulder, together at the top of the spine and finally, on the crown of your head.

❏ Allow them to fly off.

Now you are ready to contact your angel.

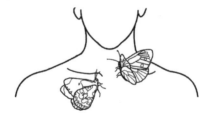

Stage 2

❏ Open your eyes and look towards the light source (though not directly at the sun).

❏ Very slowly close your eyes and ask that you may see or sense your angel.

❏ Even more slowly, half-open your eyes and you may see a misty presence framed against the light. This is transmitted from your clairvoyant, or spiritual, vision, which can perceive these higher energy vibrations.

❏ Continue to slowly close and half-open your eyes and allow the image to become clearer.

❏ If you can see nothing, keep your eyes closed and allow the image to appear on the inner screen of your mind.

❐ Now open your eyes but hold this picture in your mind for the rest of the exercise.

Stage 3

❐ With eyes open, cross your arms over your chest so that you touch each shoulder with the opposite hand.

❐ Talk to your angel as though you were saying an informal prayer, about your dreams, your hopes, your needs and sorrows. Ask the angel to keep you safe from all physical harm while you sleep and while you wake, and to protect you from all negativity.

❐ Lower your arms and touch your heart with your power hand, the one you write with.

❐ Ask that when you touch your heart in this way, wherever you are, your angel will give you a signal that he or she is close.

❐ Remain perfectly still and the signal will come, whether a sense of chill followed by warmth, a flutter like feathers against your cheek, a brush of gossamer wings enfolding you, a particular fragrance or the sound of silver bells. The angelic-presence signal will be different from that of your spirit guide, lighter and more subtle. In time you will know when your angel is close just as you do with you spirit guide. Sometimes both may come in time of crisis or great opportunity and your spirit guide will help you to tune in to the angelic presence if you find this is difficult for you.

❐ Finally, ask if there is a message. You may for now be filled with a sense of overwhelming peace and reassurance you last felt in childhood when you were safe and warm in bed (or how you imagine it should have felt). Usually the answer will come later. Occasionally you may be rewarded with a soft but clear voice in your ear that is your own and yet richer, calmer and one you have heard a thousand times in your dreams or on the wind.

Stage 4

❐ Thank your angel and you may sense a subtle withdrawal like gentle waves tugging back over your feet or a breeze moving away.

❐ Call your butterflies to settle on the crown of your head. Reverse Stage 1.

❐ Do not be in too much hurry to return to the world. Sit for a while in the soft light, letting the feeling of peace remain within you.

The angel in the crystal

Dr John Dee, the astrologer to the court of Elizabeth I, called upon angels in his crystal sphere, which was dark obsidian. However, for making contact with your personal angel I would recommend a clear crystal sphere, or ball. Clear quartz crystal is considered the most perfect stone in all cultures: the Chinese called it 'essence of the dragon', the Australian Aboriginals 'the living spirit' and the Ancient Greeks 'frozen light'.

The sphere is the geometric shape of perfection and is a symbol of eternity and immortality. Combine the two and you have a fit medium for connecting with angels. The sphere need not be large. Choose or ask for one by mail order with crystal inclusions or inner cleavages and formations that stimulate the physical eye to identify pictures within it. These images can then be amplified and interpreted by the clairvoyant eye.

Working with a crystal sphere is an effective way of getting to know your special angel better, as the sphere acts as a constant focus for the angelic vision even when your inner vision fades.

You can use quite bright light for your sphere. Hold your crystal so that you can see reflected in it brilliant moonlight or sunlight, casting sunbeams and rainbows from within. If you want to see your angel in the sphere on a dull day, light a horseshoe of small gold candles, and on a cloudy night use silver ones. Hold your crystal so that the candlelight shimmers through it. If you are working indoors, light floral incense, and outdoors work near fragrant flowers.

☐ Keep revolving the sphere slowly between your hands, pausing as you look within from different angles.

☐ There may be a natural angel formation within the sphere. If not, allow your mind to combine different lines and flashes of light so that one appears.

☐ Breathe slowly and deeply, and with each exhaled breath, visualise the light expanding so that the angel fills the crystal and then moves beyond it.

☐ Focus on a spot between the wings and allow the image of the angel to build outwards and upwards so that your angel stands in front of you, perhaps holding the sphere. You will become aware of many more details. The angel may be human height, perhaps taller and shining but never frightening or overwhelming.

☐ Talk to your angel and if you sense the time is right, very gently touch the edge of its robe or wings with your outstretched hands. Even if the place you touch fades, you will experience waves of rainbow colours and a rippling sensation through your hands.

❑ Once more, ask if there is a message or lesson you need to learn. Do not be disappointed if you have to wait for an answer. It will come in a form you readily understand in your dreams or perhaps as a symbol.

❑ In case the answer does come in symbolic form, look once more into the crystal and write down or draw whatever symbol/s you are aware of.

❑ When you have finished your dialogue, thank the angel and the presence will fade, leaving extra brilliance and occasionally sparks of light within and around the crystal.

❑ Wash the crystal under running water or splash it with water you have left in sunlight from dawn to noon (you can make a supply of this and keep it bottled in the fridge).

Keep the crystal wrapped in white silk when not in use. If you contacted your angel by moonlight, place it under your pillow while you sleep.

If you did not get a message in your dreams you may see your symbol from the crystal in actuality the next day.

This might be a strange bird you have never before seen in the garden, a large, unusual moth or butterfly that settles on you or follows you around, or a flower that blooms unexpectedly in the wrong season.

At such a sign your mind will be filled with understanding of your message, so silently thank your angel again and make your special sign of connection (see page 51).

Using small crystals to talk to angels

Within the palms of the hands are small energy centres called 'chakras' that are directly linked to the heart chakra, or centre. The heart centre is the gateway to the higher, more ethereal dimensions, so your hands can both receive angelic wisdom and transmit healing from higher sources (see page 120).

Certain crystals have traditionally been associated with angelic communication. Some are very special, the kind you might choose for a birthday, but many are quite cheap and easily obtainable.

By holding a small crystal in both hands, you can pick up angelic messages and wisdom via your fingertips and palms using a psychic process called 'psychometry', an extension of the physical sense of touch. When you have chosen a crystal, keep it in a special purse or pouch and only take it out when you wish to communicate with your angel.

If you need angelic inspiration during the day and you are busy, wherever you are, close out the world by holding the crystal.

Children may like a small angel crystal to keep under their pillow or on a bedside table to keep away fears and bad dreams.

☐ Sit quietly in your special place. Before using a crystal, light a sandalwood, pine or orange incense stick and with the smoke write over the crystal three times:

   May angels protect me.

☐ Leave the incense to burn through as you hold the crystal.

☐ If you cannot use incense you can hold the crystal under running water before use.

☐ Cup your hands round the crystal and close your eyes.

☐ If there is a specific question, ask it, or request that wisdom or help comes in whatever way you need it.

☐ Close your eyes and relax. Let any emotions or fears flow away and, if necessary, picture yourself dropping petals continuously into a flowing stream until your hands are empty.

☐ Let sensations, images and words or a sense of peace and certainty that all will be well come into your mind without forcing them.

☐ When you feel calm, even if you do not receive a direct message, thank your angel and leave the crystal in whatever source of light there is available for 30 minutes to recharge it. Then return it to the pouch.

Crystals for angelic communication

The following crystals are the best for angelic communication.

Angelite: Soft blue and opaque, veined with wings.

Aqua aura: Transparent electric blue.

Blue chalcedony: Opaque and soft blue.

Celestite: Semi-transparent blue, like ice.

Cobalt titanium aura: These are wonderful crystals for working with angels. They are in brilliant shades of royal blue, violet and gold and are able to connect us with not only guardian angels but also higher beings and archangels.

Diamond or Herkimer diamond: Clear and brilliant.

Opal aura: Translucent white that shimmers with rainbows.

Pearls: Called 'angel's tears of compassion for the suffering of humanity', these are so good when you are really sad.

Phantom quartz: This is a clear quartz crystal that has grown around an inner quartz crystal that stopped growing. This can also be used for work with nature spirits (especially when containing green chlorite) and for contacting family ancestors (see also page 21).

Quartz crystal: A clear quartz crystal in any form can be used, but especially as what is called a channelling crystal. This sort has seven edges surrounding the large, sloping face.

Rainbow quartz: This is a clear quartz but with prismatic fractures within the crystal, so when light catches the fractures, it forms rainbows.

Selenite: This is either semi-transparent or gleaming with satin stripes of white light called 'satin spar', and is excellent as a sphere.

Spirit quartz: This is a very special and newly discovered quartz crystal covered with very tiny crystals that act as a psychic trigger to angelic experiences. You will often find that your spiritual awareness is increased simply by holding it or keeping it near where you sleep.

Higher spirit guides

Once you have made connection with your angels, you have quite naturally moved your spiritual awareness up a notch. You may now begin to access wise teachers with whom you have spiritual kinship or whose wisdom will be of special help to you. These are of a higher level than those teachers you met earlier along with your spirit guides and who helped you develop specific gifts.

These are the ones who can help you to become a wiser person, to develop healing powers and perhaps to explore different spiritual paths of knowledge that belong to older traditions. These are not the ascended masters (see page 116) – the teachers who inspired humanity, like Buddha or some of the saints; these you may meet once or twice if you are very lucky as the years pass and your spirituality grows.

You may not meet your wise teacher until you are ready emotionally and until you have the time and space in your life. Those who play spiritual one-upmanship (and I meet many 'my guides are more elevated than your guides' types) are usually talking to their own ego. Don't force the pace, and one day the time will be right, perhaps in a few weeks or months after you start working fully with your angel. If you are already on the spiritual path, you may be able to access the wise guardian straight away. But for some people it may be years, if ever, before they will want to move on to the next stage.

Your spirit guide will be on hand if you get invited to attend a master-class with one of these teachers, just as your parents took you to school on the first day. These classes usually occur in your dreams or after meditation (see pages 40 and 57).

Working with the guardians

Your wise guardian may be a Native North American medicine man or woman or a Viking seiö, a senior clanswoman who lived apart or perhaps with a sister. She would obtain knowledge by channelling spirits and would be responsible for healing the clan. You may also be guided by a spá-kona or völva, who would divine future paths of individuals or the whole clan. You may meet a Celtic druid or druidess, an abbot or abbess or, if you love healing, a Chinese doctor or a wise woman herbalist. The difference between these and the teachers you met in the previous chapter is one of degree. They may have lived once or several times but have now spent much time in earthly terms perfecting their knowledge in the realms of spirit.

You can be sure the teacher-guide you need will appear, even if it is not the one you were expecting. Once you have established contact, he or she will come to you in dreams and meditation and will guide you to those earthly places and sources of wisdom that will be of most use. So if you unexpectedly end up in the British Museum when you thought you were going shopping or sightseeing, and a book is open on a table or a new exhibition draws your eye, you can be sure your teacher has work for you to do.

You may find yourself watching a television programme you would not have thought remotely interesting or a friend may give you a leaflet about a course. This happened to David, as I described in the previous chapter, when he understood, through a television programme, a healing remedy he had been shown in a dream. The only difference is that now these higher guides will be less concerned with your personal health and welfare (no good moaning to them about a headache or PMS and that you want to stop for coffee and cakes). They will open your mind to the kind of learning that will take you onwards and upwards through your spiritual path.

Using meditation to connect with your higher spirit teachers

You can also use this method to talk to your guardian angel. Specify in your mind before beginning whether it is your wise teacher or guardian angel you will try to connect with during a particular meditation.

If you have ever sat by a fountain and been filled with a sense of peace, watched a beautiful sunset, or gazed into a crystal or a deep pool, you have experienced meditative states already. Watch a child totally absorbed by a butterfly or a flower or colouring an intricate design, or humming as she sits in the sunshine, and you will witness an advanced form of meditation.

Meditation is not a chore, but a joy and a wonder. If you find, as I used to, that the formal instructions and techniques hindered rather than helped, begin meditation work by sitting in a place of natural beauty or powerful earth energies, perhaps near an old standing stone or on a spot known for its magic. By shutting out the daily world and clearing inner mental chatter, you can open the channels of the mind though which we can tune in to the higher energies of nature and the universe, the wisdom of devas (see pages 88–90 and 116–17), angels and spirit guides.

Beginning meditation

Work by your own rhythm and not by the clock. When you feel the outer world returning, don't fight it. You will quite spontaneously increase the length of your meditation times the more you practise, but this is not in direct proportion to the quality.

☐ Sit in your special place, as for relaxation, either by the light of a lavender-, rose- or sandalwood-fragranced candle or in natural daylight or moonlight. Dawn and sunset are especially favourable times.

☐ Sit comfortably on cushions or a chair so your back is supported. It is no good doing a lotus position or sitting cross-legged if you are going to get cramp or feel uncomfortable.

☐ Choose a single focus, perhaps a beautiful golden flower, a large, clear crystal sphere or amethyst geode, a tall, white pillar candle or a small water feature, and play soft music to still your mind. Always use the same focus to connect with your guardian.

☐ Start by relaxing using the butterfly technique (see page 50).

☐ Then breathe very gently and rhythmically, focusing on your breaths, while looking at the object through half-closed eyes and allowing your own boundaries to soften so that you become one with the focus. This state is the opposite of the fierce concentration you use, for example, when you are trying to stay awake to finish an assignment or to keep checking the map on a long journey.

☐ Gradually the breathing will become automatic as your full attention is centred on the focus. If troublesome thoughts emerge, allow each to form like a huge bubble and then disperse.

☐ Some people sway slightly at the beginning, to establish fluidity, and certainly you should not feel you cannot move a muscle or blink. Let the body take care of itself.

Encountering your guardian

☐ After a few minutes, you may want to close your eyes and visualise the focus all around, enclosing and protecting you.

☐ Merge with the focus so that you are the flowing water or the crystal that has formed in volcanic fire, on windy mountains, washed by millennia of rain seeping into the rock.

☐ Don't try to imagine your guardian or force the connection. Perhaps in this first session you may suddenly receive an image of the teacher, a general impression or hear a voice. If not, continue with the experience to its natural conclusion.

❑ When you are ready and can feel the external world returning, move away from the focus in your mind and concentrate once more on your gentle regular breathing. Then open your eyes if you closed them and sit still for as long as you wish.

❑ Finish by stretching like a cat after sleep.

Usually after two or three sessions, the focus will act as a doorway through which your guardian will emerge. Some people experience this the first time.

As your sessions progress, so the connection with the guardian teacher will occur sooner during the meditation and become more vivid. Remember the process for you is entirely passive and you do not need to ask questions or enter a dialogue. Just get used to the presence and perhaps absorb words or images that are sent to you.

Sometimes you may seem to get little that is tangible, but you are probably receiving strength, healing of hidden issues in your life and deeper understanding, so just let things flow.

Keep these sessions to about twice a week, as they are spiritually very intense and wisdom will come to you in other ways between times, especially in dreams.

Channelling the wisdom using automatic writing

Now comes the part you have been waiting for – the knowledge. Automatic writing is a technique we will use a number of times during the book, as it is an effective way of expressing wisdom transmitted from higher sources. You are not calling up spirits, nor are your body or mind possessed by them. The pen is operated by the same power, called 'psychokinesis' (mind movement), as when you use a pendulum. You can put the pen down at any time. You can also use this method to receive wisdom from your guardian angel if that was the focus of the meditation.

❑ Sit quietly after your meditation with a pen in your hand and a few sheets of white paper. Keep the same pen for all your channelling.

❑ You may feel your writing hand tremble slightly when you are ready to start writing.

❑ Don't ask any questions or try to force the words. If they don't come, leave them for another time.

❏ Usually, however, you will find that you do start writing quite spontaneously. You may write a few lines or several pages. When you sense the words are no longer flowing, stop.

❏ Read your words. They may suggest ways to increase your wisdom, or provide information about the background of your guardian or perhaps the realms he or she now occupies. They may be answers to issues that have puzzled you or encouragement and advice about matters you find difficult.

When you have time, copy the key parts of the channelling into your spirit journal. Over the weeks you will see how the teaching is progressing and perhaps how you are moving in a new direction. Add also to your journal teaching that comes from dreams or from the external world.

What if I change my mind?

Situations change and you may enter a really busy or stressful time in your life, become ill or tired. Your spiritual journey should always be a pleasure (if hard work) and never a chore or burden. If you don't want to meditate, study healing or do more than check in with your guides and angel periodically, go with your instinct. You can take a break at any time, just as with an earthly course. Just tell your spirit guide you want some time out and your wise teacher will step back until you are ready to go on. You will continue to interact with your guardian angel and spirit guides. You may still see your wise teacher from time to time in dreams but this will be like greeting an older wise person who is checking on your well-being and may be offering a pointer in the right direction.

You have in no way failed if you realise you want to go slower or that you do not want to study healing formally or learn the secrets of the universe. It is not a cosmic race and some people are happy, having looked into higher realms of learning, to carry on at their own earlier, slower spiritual pace. They do good to friends and family and fulfil their earthly demands and this is quite as valid as sitting on a hillside meditating while the cat is yowling for food and the bills are unpaid. You have an eternity of time, so be patient with yourself.

5

Developing your spiritual energies to tune in to higher dimensions

In the previous chapters I have written about meeting your most significant guides and guardians, who exist on different spiritual planes. Angels and wise teachers became more accessible after you had strengthened communication with your own spirit guide and helper guardians.

There are other spirit guides and guardians that you can encounter with very little spiritual training, including the spirits of the natural world and your own deceased relatives, who may return on family occasions or to offer reassurance. These I have written about in the following two chapters before we ascend spiritually towards the lofty archangels, shining nature devas and master teachers.

First it might be useful, now you are encountering spirit beings and dimensions regularly, if I describe the different levels of spiritual energies within your own spiritual-energy field, or aura. The higher levels of aura energy are the gateways to higher spiritual planes and their inhabitants.

As you work, over weeks and months, with spirit guides and angels, so your connection with your own higher aura energies spontaneously evolves and you become aware of more elevated beings.

Our spirit form

We all carry within our physical body a spirit, or etheric, body that survives after death and has been described either as a silver essence or as a double of our physical body at its peak. When you see your spirit guide, he or she appears in their spirit body, the form they took on Earth when they were most fit and vital. If you are visited by an elderly deceased relative, he or she will look quite young again because you are seeing the spirit body. This existed all the time within the physical body on Earth, but now houses the soul and essential self for eternity.

We are spiritual beings in an earthly body. I have said that before. Of course, our spirit and earthly bodies occupy the same space, our external physical form, while we are alive. However, the inner body is not packed with flesh and organs, but is altogether lighter and brighter, made of pure energy. This inner spirit body is a mass of swirling rainbow colours and, because it is so filled with energy, extends beyond the limits of the physical body as a rainbow-energy field. This external rainbow-energy field is called our 'aura', or psychic-energy field, and connects with the auras of other people's spirit bodies. (See my book *Chakra Power for Healing and Harmony*, Foulsham/Quantum, 2001) for more on this.

Of course, the aura can get polluted by external noise and toxins, and by general negativity. If our physical body is exhausted or ill, that is reflected in a much duller and visibly small external aura. Equally our inner emotions and harmony or turmoil of our physical mind affect the brightness of the aura. But that is another book.

The spiritual senses

It is not our physical eyes that see this aura field, but our clairvoyant vision. The clairvoyant, or inner psychic, eye, which enables us to see the aura of others or ourselves in a mirror and to perceive spirit beings, is the spirit body's version of the physical body's sense of sight.

Our claraudient, or inner psychic, ear, which enables us to hear sounds from the non-physical world, is the spirit body's version of our physical ear. Our clairsentient powers, the ability to detect unearthly sensations, for example the perfume of a deceased grandmother, and gain impressions about old places intuitively, is an extension of our physical taste and smell.

Finally there is psychometry, the sense of psychic touch, which enables us to pick up spiritual information through our fingertips. We experience it also in the form of psychokinesis, where the mind controls hand movements during automatic writing or when using a pendulum. This is an extension of physical touch.

These psychic senses, which we have already worked with in earlier chapters, help you to become more aware of, and communicate with, progressively higher spiritual beings and enable you to tune in to non-physical planes of existence more easily.

Physical versus spirit body

As children we can switch instantly from the physical mind/body level to a spiritual level of operating. As we get older, our conscious mind becomes increasingly important for processing essential information. The spiritual aspect and spirit body is relegated to specific times, such as during worship or meditation, or when a sudden crisis or family bereavement occurs and we can no longer believe that the physical body and mind are infallible. In spiritual work the spirit body takes predominance.

Of course, we still need the physical mind in spiritual experience to understand what we are doing, to absorb, categorise, record and make sense of what we have learned from our spirit guides and to teach others. We need our physical senses to enable us to make connection with different kinds and colours of crystals, to feel and see externally the movement of a pendulum, to smell different earthly flowers so we can differentiate between and categorise non-earthly scents. Especially at first, we use our voices to pray or to talk aloud to spiritual beings or a deceased relative and our hands to write down or draw the messages we receive from spirits.

Later in the chapter I will write about how the two bodies are linked through the chakras, or psychic energy centres, in the body, but first let's continue with the concept of the aura, or energy field, and how its levels link with spiritual planes.

About the aura

The individual aura forms the connecting point for the interchange of energies between people, animals and plants and the earth and, most importantly for spirit-guide work, with the cosmos and cosmic beings. This spiritual bio-energetic aura field varies in size and density under different conditions and is estimated to extend between 2 centimetres and a metre (1 inch to about three feet). It surrounds the body as an ellipse. Gautama Buddha's aura was said to extend, and therefore to influence people, over a range of several miles.

Aura colours, too, can alter according to conditions, and may be observed clairvoyantly as radiating, intermingling and swirling bands of colour.

The spiritual energy bands that make up the aura become progressively less dense and more ethereal the further from the physical body they extend. The outermost levels, in blue, indigo and violet are the highest spiritually; finally, beyond the aura our spiritual energies merge, as pure white light, with the cosmos. These higher levels are always there, and in childhood are frequently used. In adulthood the higher external levels

63

are like rooms whose lights we hardly ever switch on because we don't visit them; but they are still there, and through spiritual work you can switch on those lights and enter those rooms.

Beginning where you are

Even if you have never done spiritual work before reading this or any other book on spirituality, the innermost three layers of your aura are all sufficiently sensitive to enable you to become spontaneously aware, for example, of nature spirits. They may also, perhaps, occasionally, at times of great emotion in your life, connect you with your deceased grandparents, as well as your own personal guide and guardian angel.

The more you work with spirit beings or carry out any other form of spiritual work, the more levels of aura you automatically switch on, or activate. It then becomes easier to communicate with those spiritual beings you may have already been vaguely aware of, perhaps spontaneously. As a bonus of your increasingly sensitised aura you can then tune in to even more elevated spiritual beings that live on still higher planes of existence.

Moving through the aura levels into different planes of existence is like learning a foreign language when you want to spend time in a new country. Gradually you speak, understand and even think in this foreign language instead of just parroting phrases from an elementary phrase book. Once you are versed in the real vocabulary of your new land, whether a holiday destination or a spirit plane, you interact with the residents and can share a little more knowledge of their lives.

Interpreting the levels and the spiritual planes

Seven is the linking number. There are seven levels of the aura that represent, and are the visible part of, the seven levels of the spirit body. In this chapter I have focused on the essential aura levels rather than exploring the nature of the spirit body in detail.

There are also seven planes of existence and seven chakras, or psychic-energy centres, linking the spirit and physical body. These chakra points can be used to energise the different layers of the aura and so increase your ability to work with different planes of existence.

How far can you evolve spiritually? If you can learn to operate through, say, the blue-aura level of your spirit body, then obviously your awareness of spiritual dimensions will be greater and more rewarding than if you were still at the lower, orange level.

Emanuel Swedenborg, the eighteenth-century scientist, Christian mystic and visionary, who incidentally believed we all have two guardian angels, taught that all people are born with the spiritual potential to become angels, whatever their religion. If they choose the path of virtue, they can continue on an angelic path after death. This is different from the conventional view that angels never lived. However, it does emphasise the concept that we all contain the spark of divinity within us, the seed of the highest spiritual level, and so we can experience other dimensions during life.

The seven-level system

A number of psychic researchers believe that the seven planes of existence are like the seven aura and spirit-body levels contained within the same space – in this case, the universe. Of course, the higher planes, like the higher levels of the aura, extend far wider than the lower ones, and the highest have no limits. There are not separate areas in the sky marked, for example, 'Archangels only'. The more evolved you become spiritually the more you realise that angels are everywhere. Certainly children seem able to tune in to spiritual beings in the most crowded street or tiny city garden.

Some of the names seem confusing; for example, the Astral layer of the aura is the fourth level of the aura and is different from the Astral plane, which is the second spiritual plane. The name of the first layer of the aura, the Etheric layer, is also very confusing, since 'etheric' is also applied to the whole etheric, or spirit, body. The Etheric layer refers here to just one layer of the aura.

So take each name in the context it is used. In practice the names don't matter much. It is the ideas that are important.

The Etheric layer and the Earth plane

This first aura level is powered by the red base or root chakra, or psychic-body energy centre (see page 74). It fits almost like a second skin, extending from just under a centimetre to 5 centimetres (½ to 2 inches) from the body. This layer is most closely linked to the condition of the physical body on which it is superimposed, following the outline of the physical form. It usually appears initially as silver light or haze but when the root chakra, or energy centre, is functioning fully, this aura level may be seen as red.

The Etheric layer is linked with the Earth plane. The Earth plane is the one closest to Mother Earth, on which we walk. On a physical level it is the physical space our bodies occupy. But we are focusing on the spiritual plane that is superimposed on the physical earth.

During life, the etheric, or human spirit, body can most easily visit the first and most accessible spirit plane during sleep or out-of-body experiences. This plane is the level of dreams and meditation and is the vibrational level at which you first catch glimpses of spirit guides, angels and wise teachers, in dreams and through prayer and meditation. However, direct communication is hard, because most of them operate on a higher spiritual level.

One exception is your personal spirit guide. Though your personal guide no longer lives on the Earth plane, he or she is able to slow their spiritual vibrations right down so they can talk to you through your mind and psychic senses, for example using fragrance as a link. Your spirit physician and teacher will also be able to communicate with you mainly through sleep and signs and symbols.

Your doorkeeper will protect you even at this level, though he comes from the higher, fourth level of existence.

The Emotional layer and the Astral plane

The second layer of the aura is powered by the orange, sacral chakra. The aura at this level appears as orange light and is usually seen as a swirling mass of energy about the body following the human shape. It is not as clearly defined as the Etheric layer. In fact, each layer moving outwards from the body becomes less and less structured. This is the layer that deals with desires and emotions and, not surprisingly, is most affected by mood variations.

The Emotional layer is linked with the Astral plane. 'Astral' comes from the Latin word for star. This is the level of your aura and spiritual awareness at which you first see non-human guides who have an independent existence.

The entry point is imagination or visualisation, and children spend a lot of time visiting the Astral plane. Unlike your spirit guide, many spirit beings here will not actively seek your company unless they become aware you are tuned in and receptive. They include fairies and nature spirits and the wise animals whose wisdom the Native North Americans value so much. The latter tend to be more helpful to newcomers to this plane.

Young people in the Australian Aboriginal and Native North American traditions would go out into the wilderness as part of their initiation ceremony into adulthood. After fasting and sleep deprivation they would make contact with a wise animal, who would act as their guide.

This is also the level of mythological archetypes or universal symbols, visited by shamans, the magicians/priests/healers from a tradition that has existed for thousands of years among indigenous tribes from Australia to Siberia. These are the realms told about in fairy stories.

Once you work deliberately with this level (see pages 79–94), you can not only communicate with powerful helper creatures but also visit and learn from these mythological realms through lucid dreams and through mind travel or guided visualisations. Lucid dreams involve becoming aware of when you are dreaming and using this knowledge to explore the Astral plane (see page 129).

You are now able to initiate contact with your spirit and helper guides more directly.

The Mental layer and the Rainbow plane

The third level of the aura is powered by the golden-yellow solar plexus chakra. It is usually most visible around the head and shoulders as a yellowish light. It is in this layer that thoughts are translated into action. Developed further and extended through ritual, it becomes the stuff of magical spells.

The Mental layer is linked to the Rainbow plane. This plane is akin to our idea of heaven and is where your deceased family and ancestors live. It is said they fashion from their thoughts the kind of lives they wish to live, right down to their homes. They may return on family occasions such as the birth of a baby, like any mortal grandparent, and are available to guide family members, so you may experience their presence, even on the Earth plane, especially in dreams.

Love is so strong that a deceased loved one will hear your call for help and send reassurance, perhaps in the form of a dream or by transmitting earthly perfume or some sign by which you will know they are with you.

Once you become aware of this level then you can communicate more easily not only with immediate relatives but also with your ancestors. You may begin to have personal past-life experiences or link in to those of your ancestors, and may be able to interpret messages from other people's deceased relatives, through the gift of mediumship (see page 100).

You will be assisted by your spirit guide and may become aware of a variety of teachers and helpers, sometimes even without needing to ask your spirit guide. This ability develops more on the next level.

The Astral layer and the Buddhic plane

The green, heart chakra rules the fourth aura layer, which divides the three lower and personally orientated bodies from those that link to higher dimensions. This is the layer of spiritual love, and is seen as a rich green, and sometimes, if your love is directed towards healing, pink, aura. This is the level at which you can channel healing energies from higher planes, not least through the minor chakras in the palms of your hands, and by using crystals and automatic writing to channel information about permanent relationships. Bibliomancy, finding information from books you just chance to see or open, is but one method; another is meditation.

The Astral layer is linked with the Buddhic plane. Here you will meet spirit guides who either have never lived or are wise mortals who have decided to devote themselves after life to teaching and guiding mortals on Earth. Here will be your guardian angels and wise teachers such as Native North American medicine men and women and Viking wise women.

At this level comes knowledge of the wisdom of past worlds, and you may be drawn to a particular form of spirituality.

The three higher layers of the body/spirit planes

These aura levels replicate the three lower ones but at a higher level of vibration. They are the seat of the higher self, and some regard them as forming the soul. When we utilise this level of our being we can more easily commune with beings of higher spiritual orders.

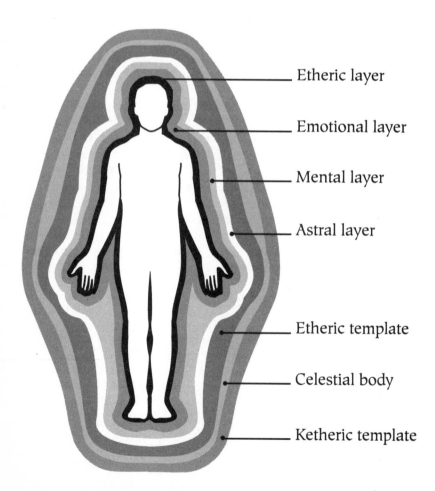

Etheric layer

Emotional layer

Mental layer

Astral layer

Etheric template

Celestial body

Ketheric template

The Etheric template and the Atmic plane

The sky-blue throat chakra controls this fifth level, which is blue, and is a copy of the physical body on a higher spiritual vibration. Some see this level of functioning as triggering awareness of the essential self that enables the spirit body to detach itself at will. This is the level at which the collective unconscious or cosmic memory bank can be accessed, and the boundaries of time lose their meaning at this gateway.

Healers at this level have a blue light round them when they heal and often use their voice as well as their hands. It may take many months or even years to work spontaneously at this level.

The Etheric template links with the Atmic plane. Here the archangels, saints, devas (those shining beings who ensure the blueprints of nature are put into action), the master and mistress healers and the ascended masters and beings of light may be found.

If you regularly carry out archangel rituals or try to channel from light beings, using crystal geodes or higher meditation techniques (see pages 104 and 117), awareness of the guardians of this plane increases. Ritual, as well as astral or out-of-body travel through crystal geodes, offers entry points, as do patience and finding inner stillness.

The Celestial body and the Anupadaka plane

The indigo third eye, or brow, chakra fuels this sixth layer of the aura. This aura level may be perceived as diffuse indigo light. Emotions are now focused on global concerns and you may find that you become less concerned with specific spiritual techniques and more with receiving wisdom from every source. This aura level reflects the blueprint, or ideal, of your lower emotional aura. Your words will spontaneously become increasingly wise and prophetic and you will see the spirit guides and angels of other people very clearly. This ability may begin on the previous level.

The Celestial body links with the Anupadaka plane. On this plane we are able to communicate with personal aspects of cosmic energies. Here are the highest orders of angels who guard the veil between this and the next unknowable level, the Holy family, and various deity forms who make up aspects of the separate God or Goddess in different religions and ages. For example, there is Parvati, the Hindu wise and gentle wife of Shiva, the father god, and Isis, the beautiful Ancient Egyptian mother goddess of the moon and magic. (See page 135 for more about this plane.)

Prayer, offerings, incense-burning and ritual may help us to glimpse this plane.

The Ketheric template and the Adi plane

The crown chakra controls this seventh layer, and it may take several years before you are sufficiently spiritually evolved to fully work with these energies. Its colour is violet, merging into pure white or gold. It is also known as the 'Causal body'. This is the highest layer of the spiritual level. Through this layer we can hope, perhaps after many lifetimes, to one day become one with the cosmos, with pure spirit or divinity. At the point of death, a dying person may report brilliant light and subsequently relatives may see the spirit leaving the body as pure white light. It is hypothesised this one glimpse of pure divinity will carry them through the fear of death.

The Ketheric template links with the Adi plane. The highest of the seven planes, this is the realm of divinity of the God or Goddess as one undifferentiated power, complete oneness. This is not really attainable, but as we become more evolved, one of our higher guides may show us the threshold (see pages 135–6). We can also occasionally approach this level as a peak, or mystical, experience, when we have a sudden moment of pure ecstasy and illumination.

Perceiving the seven aura levels

One of the ways of increasing your awareness of spiritual beings is to focus on the seven aura levels in ascending order and at each speak to one of the guides or wise beings whose energies represent that level of spiritual vibration. Try this now, even though you have only worked with a limited range of guardians so far in the book.

❑   Sit in front of a wide-angled mirror – a free-standing full-length looking glass is ideal.

☐ Arrange in front of you seven candles in the seven rainbow colours in a horseshoe shape so that the colours can be seen within the mirror as well in actuality.

☐ To the far left have the red candle, then the orange, and moving down the horseshoe shape, the yellow and the green in front of you at the bottom of the horseshoe formation, then going to the right and outwards up the horseshoe shape the blue, indigo and finally, to the far right, violet.

☐ Light the red candle first and switch off all other lights.

☐ Focus first on the red candle. See its light as a hoop of colour encircling you.

☐ Visualise, and then greet in your own words, a guardian from the first Earth plane, your own spirit guide, waiting to lead you through the aura pathway.

☐ Light the orange candle and visualise the swirling colour surrounding the red.

☐ Picture and greet a guardian from the second, Astral plane, the fairy or nature spirit level. For each colour you may experience different emotions and sensations.

☐ Light the yellow candle and see the yellow lights swirling around the orange and red aura layers surrounding you.

☐ Visualise and greet a guardian from the Rainbow plane, perhaps a well-loved deceased grandparent or an ancestor.

☐ Light the green candle and picture the green light swirling around the other colours now in your aura.

☐ Picture and greet a guardian from the Buddhic plane, your guardian angel or a wise teacher from an ancient tradition.

☐ Light next your blue candle and let the blue light form the outer layer of your aura.

☐ Picture and greet a guardian from the Atmic plane, an archangel or saint.

☐ Light your indigo candle and allow the light to swirl around the outer limits of your aura.

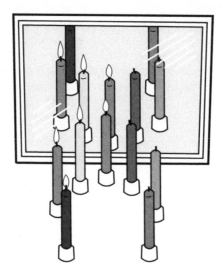

- ❏ Visualise and greet a guardian from the Anupadaka plane, your favourite god or goddess form or a brilliant golden angel.

- ❏ Finally, light the violet candle and watch that forming a swirling mist around your aura, merging with pure white light.

- ❏ Picture a midnight-blue veil with golden stars on it and, beyond that, brilliance filtering through, and ask that one day you will see that light.

- ❏ Sit for a while in the candlelight to strengthen your own aura, leaving you energised but calm, and let any messages from higher realms filter, for now, through your spirit guide or guardian angel.

- ❏ When you are ready, move away and light a white candle in the centre of the mirror where you were sitting.

- ❏ Leave the candles a little longer and then blow them out sending light and thanks to your guides.

This is a good monthly method of opening your energy channels for spirit work and keeping the aura levels clear and energised.

The chakras and your guides

Your chakras (psychic-energy centres) are each linked, as I explained above, to one of the aura levels and so to one of the planes of existence. They are also the connection between your physical and spiritual body and penetrate all seven levels of your spirit body simultaneously.

Most traditions locate chakras vertically along the axis of the body, either on or just in front of the backbone; however, they are linked with and take their name from locations on the front of the body, such as the navel, heart, throat and brow. They also penetrate the axis of the spirit body.

From above, the universal life-force, or prana, is filtered via psychic channels, or nadirs, down the chakra system, entering through the chakra at the crown of the head. As this pure white or golden life-force flows in and downwards, each chakra transforms the energy into an appropriate form.

Red root light flows upwards from the Earth via the root or base chakra from beneath our feet (see diagram below).

But the energy does not flow through a single channel only. The same light force is flowing into the individual chakras through the aura all around the body through the chakra connections. This means we are beings of light. Of course, the chakras also energise (but can also block) the aura, and each chakra energises its own aura level.

Therefore by keeping your chakras free flowing and healthy you can make your spirit-guide work easier as energy flows in its many directions.

You can energise your spirit body through your physical one or vice versa, for example, when you apply crystals to your physical body or move a pendulum above your chakras without making contact with the physical body (see pages 77–8). The effect on your aura is the same.

I have repeated below the aura/spirit body and spirit plane links from the previous section, as these connections are complex but important.

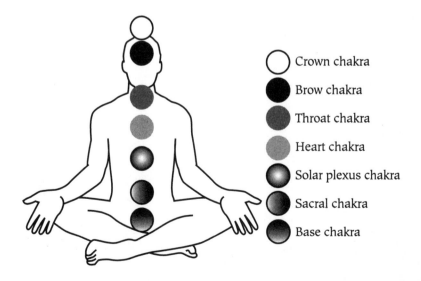

Crown chakra

Brow chakra

Throat chakra

Heart chakra

Solar plexus chakra

Sacral chakra

Base chakra

The base or root chakra

Layer (aura): Etheric.

Plane: Earth.

Colour: Red.

Crystals: Bloodstone, garnet, red jasper, lodestone, obsidian, ruby, smoky quartz, black tourmaline.

This is the chakra of the Earth and it draws its beautiful, deep red light upwards from the Earth through the feet, and through our perineum when we sit on the ground. Both these are points at which the root chakra can be accessed and energised. The minor chakras in the soles of the feet are also ruled by and connected directly to the root.

It is linked with the kundalini, or serpent energy, which in Eastern philosophy is described as coiled at the base of the spine and which provides the driving power for the chakra system.

The root rules the legs, feet and skeleton, including the teeth and the large intestine.

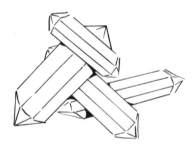

The sacral chakra

Layer (aura): Emotional.

Plane: Astral.

Colour: Orange.

Crystals: Banded orange agate, amber, aquamarine, orange calcite, carnelian, coral, fluorite, rutilated quartz, moonstone.

This is the chakra of the Moon and Water. It is seated in the sacrum and lower abdomen, around the reproductive system, and focuses on all aspects of physical comfort or satisfaction. It controls the blood, all bodily fluids and hormones, the reproductive system, kidneys, circulation and bladder, and is a chakra especially sensitive to stress and imbalance if our natural cycles are out of harmony.

The solar plexus chakra

Layer (aura): Mental.

Plane: Rainbow.

Colour: Yellow.

Crystals: Golden beryl, yellow calcite, citrine, desert rose, tiger's eye, topaz.

This is the chakra of Fire. You will find the third chakra above the navel around the stomach area or, in some systems, further up towards the central cavity of the lungs. It controls digestion, the liver, spleen, gall bladder, stomach and small intestine, and the metabolism.

The heart chakra

Layer (aura): Astral.

Plane: Buddhic.

Colour: Green or pink.

Crystals: Moss agate, aventurine, amazonite, chrysoprase, emerald, jade, kunzite, rose quartz.

This is the chakra of Air or the Winds. It is situated in the centre of the chest, radiating over the heart, lungs, breasts and also the hands and arms. There are minor chakras in the palm of each hand, and these are the outlets for healing powers from the higher centres (see pages 120–22).

Compassion and transformation of our everyday lives through connection with our still centre of being result from a clear heart chakra.

The throat chakra

Layer (aura): Etheric.

Plane: Atmic.

Colour: Sky-blue.

Crystals: Blue lace agate, angelite, celestite, lapis lazuli, blue quartz, sapphire, turquoise.

This is the chakra of Sound. The throat chakra is situated close to the Adam's apple, in the centre of the neck. It controls the mouth, the neck and shoulders and the passages that run up to the ears, as well as the throat and speech organs.

The third eye, or brow, chakra

Layer (aura): Celestial.

Plane: Anupadaka.

Colour: Indigo.

Crystals: Amethyst, ametrine, azurite, fluorite, lepidolite, sodalite.

This is the chakra of Light. The brow chakra is situated just above the bridge of the nose, in the centre of the brow. It controls the eyes and ears, both hemispheres of the brain, and radiates into the central cavity of the brain.

The crown chakra

Layer (aura): Ketheric.

Plane: Adi.

Colours: Violet, merging with white or gold as rays from the cosmos pour in.

Crystals: White and purple banded amethyst, diamond, clear fluorite, pearl, clear crystal quartz, brilliant purple sugilite.

This is the chakra of Spirit or pure Aether. The crown chakra is situated at the top of the head. It extends beyond the crown, and some locate the centre about three finger-breadths above the top of the head. It rules the brain, body and psyche. In this chakra resides our personal core of divinity, which ultimately connects to the source of divinity itself.

Cleansing and energising your chakras for spirit-guide work

The link between aura and chakras is two-way. If a chakra is blocked, perhaps because of exhaustion, illness, pollution, lack of fresh air, poor diet, stress, overwork, or negativity by others, you may find that your spirit-guide work feels more of an effort, or communication is not clear.

The seven-candle method I suggested on pages 71–2 is a good way of keeping chakras as well as the aura clear because of the two-way connection. Equally, if your aura is blocked for any reason, then a blast of power from its own chakra is the fastest and most effective way of restoring vitality.

There are a number of ways you can cleanse and energise your chakras before spirit-guide work. I would advise clearing all your chakras, not just the one related to the aura level you are operating at (for example the second, Astral level, to contact fairies or nature spirits), because the energies are so connected.

Using a pendulum

Pass your hand slowly up and down your body and you will identify each chakra area by a sensation that feels as if you are holding your hand over an emptying plughole in a sink. Everyone's chakras are in a slightly different position.

The key is to allow the pendulum to follow its own pathways over the body, so just relax.

❏ Take a crystal pendulum that you have plunged into a glass of cold water. Pass it slowly 2 or 3 centimetres (about an inch) away from your body in a clockwise spiralling pattern upwards from your feet towards the crown, making sure you include all seven chakra areas.

If one of your chakras is blocked, then the pendulum will stop moving over the chakra centre.

If the chakra is overactive and spinning too fast, as sometimes happens when you are under stress or when there has been a lot of noise in your life, the pendulum will spiral anti-clockwise over the chakra and you may feel as though you have received a mild electric shock.

If all is well the pendulum will spiral clockwise steadily over all the chakras.

❏ To energise a blocked chakra, deliberately spin the pendulum anti-clockwise several times over the blocked chakra and then clockwise to energise it.

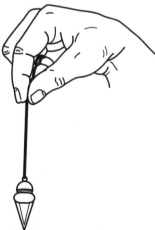

❑ An overactive chakra can be calmed by slowly and gently turning the pendulum in anti-clockwise circles till you sense the slowing energies.

❑ When you have completed the upward pendulum pathway, even if all is clear, pass the pendulum slowly clockwise nine times about three finger-breadths above the top of your head to energise the crown.

❑ Then move the pendulum clockwise slowly downwards, allowing it to spiral where it will, just above your skin, until you reach your feet.

❑ Plunge the pendulum three times into running water to cleanse it.

Using crystals

❑ Lie down and place appropriate chakra crystals over each chakra point (you can tape difficult ones in place or ask a friend to help).

❑ Use two base- or root-chakra crystals, one on each foot for the root chakra, or lie on top of a very rounded crystal placed in the small of your back.

❑ Alternatively, fill a jug of clear mineral water and add a crystal from each of the seven groups to the water.

❑ Leave the crystals in the jug for eight hours, preferably during daylight, and afterwards bottle the chakra water and use it in drinks and baths. Sprinkle some on your hair to energise the aura.

Using colour

❑ Fill a vase with seven different coloured flowers that correspond with the chakra colours (use two shades of purple or one purple and one white).

❑ Breathe in the colours as light slowly through your mouth and picture darker or misty light leaving on the out breath.

❑ Eat seven different coloured foods. Use one purple food such as grapes and one white if you cannot find two different purples. The food should be fresh and unprocessed but can be lightly cooked if necessary.

6

Working with the spirits of nature, elemental powers, nature devas and animal helpers

Before we ascend higher to the realms of the archangels and shining beings, let's spend some time on the Astral plane, which is linked to the second level of your aura, the natural world. Here we can encounter the wondrous spirit beings of childhood.

When you were young you were probably aware of the essences of nature everywhere, especially if you camped out in the forest or spent time on the shores of a lake or the sea. You were probably able to communicate in your mind with animals, even wildlife.

Anita is Norwegian but as a child lived in the centre of an English city with a tiny garden. She always talked to what she called the 'white elves' that came from a high place but played around the base of a pine tree. Years later she learned about the Scandinavian *ljossalfs*, or light elves, who lived in *Ljossalfsheim*, or Alfheim, one of the nine worlds that made up the universe on the top level of the World Tree, above the world of Midgard, where humans lived, according to Scandinavian mythology. She was lucky, because they are rarely seen by mortals, but she grew up to be a gifted healer.

The ability to see nature spirits fades as everyday life and the logical part of the mind takes over, and we perceive the Astral plane mostly in dreams. However, on a windy day, or on one of the seasonal change points, the stirring of spirit life in nature is unmistakable, especially if you have started working with a spirit guide who has reopened your channels of awareness.

Do nature spirits exist?

We know from science that even plants have animate life. Plants radiate light round their forms that can be detected in Kirlian photography, a method of capturing auras on film. Plant auras fade when they are cut or deprived of water, and if a leaf is cut from a plant, the aura, or energy field, of the missing part remains.

What is more, plants respond to unspoken threats, not only against themselves but others of their species. By hooking plants up to polygraph equipment (and later ECG and EEG equipment), Cleve Backster and other researchers experimenting during the 1960s and 70s in the United States discovered that not only do plants respond to experiences in their environment, but also they seem to be able to pick up on people's thoughts. The strongest readings obtained were in reaction to the destruction of living cells, whether they were plant, animal or human cells. The death of living cells, or even the threat of death, caused intense electromagnetic reactions by all the plants present.

The messages of the nature spirits

In this chapter I will focus on making the connection and on channelling wisdom from the wise ones in nature.

The first message from the essences of nature is about making connection with the natural world, of joy in all weathers and all seasons, even if you live and work in a city. The second is about sensitivity to the natural world, and the responsibility for its preservation. Each year an area of trees the size of Wales is cut down from the Amazonian rainforests, the lungs of the Earth.

Nature-spirit energies

One of the most powerful arguments for the existence of nature spirits is that, like angels, they have common consistent characteristics in legends in different parts of the world and in many ages, where there was no apparent geographical connection. Also, accounts of people who have reported contact with these ethereal beings extend back many hundreds of years. That would suggest that fairies may indeed possess objective reality and share the same space as we do. But because their forms exist at a higher level of vibration beyond the physical eye, we see them clairvoyantly, and so children, young people and women perceive them most readily, since they are most open to experiences through their psychic senses.

Nature spirits, who live near water, in trees or in flowers, or the gnomes, elves or dwarves of the forests, tend not to adopt a particular human, as a spirit guide will. Rather, they are attached to their own element, be it earth, air, fire or water, and may become aware that we can see or sense them. You may even, if you visit the same area of woodland or lake regularly and sit quietly, see the same creatures many times. If they are in your garden and you leave them offerings of small crumbs of bread, mixed with honey and milk, they may help you to grow beautiful plants. You may even have a small nature essence in indoor pot plants.

The messages you get may be indirect, but nevertheless they are important in opening you to connection with the realms of spirit and in bringing you harmony and real joy.

Try the following exercise to make the connection. It is one I have used and taught many times.

Go alone or with a trusted friend or one of your children who can sit quietly to a place where there are trees, bushes, flowers and grasses growing wild, in the early morning or evening, when it is very quiet.

❑ Take a notebook, a pen and coloured pencils.

❑ Sit and, even if there is not a breeze, you may detect movement among the grasses and perhaps a silvery flash of light out of the corner of your eye.

❑ Perhaps a large, colourful butterfly or dragonfly, forms in which nature spirits are often perceived, may hover around or settle close and seem unafraid.

❑ Remain still and you may hear rustlings or whisperings, quite unlike animal scuttling.

❑ Without moving your body, touch a grass or flower very lightly and you will feel the energy connection, a slight buzzing in your ear and a feeling like warm liquid trickling through your veins.

❑ Close your eyes very slowly, still maintaining connection with the plant, and in your mind the picture of an essence may take shape. It may not be what you would expect – it may not even be a recognisable form, but a swirl, a series of brightly coloured lights, or an old man or woman or a young child. You may hear words in your mind.

❑ Slowly open your eyes, still holding the plant, and you may be rewarded with a misty outline or a series of silver dots, one way our conscious eye, assisted by the clairvoyant eye, perceives nature-spirit energies.

❑ Record each fairy form immediately afterwards, not worrying about your artistic ability, but capturing the mood and the movement. Some may evoke a few lines of poetry or a song.

❑ When you have finished, sit for a while longer, and then leave a small offering in the place, such as a small crystal, a pearl button (nature spirits love shiny things) or a silver- or gold-coloured coin.

If you went with a friend or a child compare notes with what they saw. Children's experiences are always brilliant.

If you return to the site regularly, you may identify one or two fey forms and become aware as you are watching them that they are watching you. Do not expect friendship, but you may catch glimpses, as you make the psychic connection with them, of other nature spirits and of their world.

Communicating with nature spirits

Gradually you may start receiving one or two messages as you sit in your natural place, usually not about your personal life, but requests for help. Perhaps a local tree has been cut down and the nature spirits want you to find either a new sapling or a larger tree or similar species where the nature essence can go. You will be given instructions in your mind but, as a rule, a twig or stem with leaves from any plant that has been cut down before its time should be placed very close to another, stronger, specimen to help the displaced essence on its way. This will be rewarded by unexpected blessings in your own life.

You can also work with the essences in your garden and even in your indoor pot plants, which will need lots of extra nourishment and a moss- or tree-agate planted in the soil if you are drawing psychic power with them.

If you sit in the garden as evening falls or in the early morning, a firefly or moth – evening creatures – or a dragonfly or butterfly in the morning, may hover over a particular spot that may emit tiny sparkles or light-beams. Go there and you may see a tiny shoot bursting through or a herb not getting enough light or water.

If you have bought a new plant and are not sure where to site it, your attention will be drawn, perhaps in your mind, to a particularly suitable spot.

Garden pendulum power

If communication with your garden spirits seems hard, perhaps because they shun humans when overwhelmed by the noise and activity of even a rural garden, use the pendulum to amplify communication.

For planting something new, hold the pendulum first over the new plants and ask the nature spirit where it would like to live. Then stand up and follow the positive swing of the pendulum till it stops and spirals over the perfect place.

Crazy, say the sceptics. Try it and notice the improvement in your garden.

You can also hold your pendulum over a sick plant and ask a series of Yes/No questions (see page 43 for the different pendulum movements). If you spiral the pendulum first three times anti-clockwise and then three times clockwise you can send healing light into the plant to help a tired nature spirit fix things.

Office pot plants also have their own spirits. These will need special nurturing and frequent outings to your garden, or at least to a place of natural sunlight, to restore natural energies, which can grow weak when surrounded by electricity and noise.

Identifying different nature essences

Each of the nature spirits is associated with one particular element: Earth, Air, Fire and Water. Each is ruled by a particular king or queen.

Depending on where you live, you may have the opportunity to work regularly with certain kinds of nature spirits. You can supplement your experiences by seeking out nature spirits on weekends away or longer holidays to other terrains and climates. For example, if you live inland you might encounter lake spirits, but may have to wait till you visit the ocean to experience the wilder sea essences. You can supplement your work with symbols, for example the garden gnome or ceramic winged fairies in your garden or among your indoor plants.

Each element has a representative kind of nature spirit that I have listed first. You can read more about the different creatures in my key to nature spirits below or in the *Complete Guide to Fairies and Magical Beings* (Weiser/Red Wheel 2001, Piatkus 2000).

Some of the substances you use to connect with nature spirits can be used as offerings, for example milk, beer or honey.

You can also use the natural fragrance either in the plant or flower form or as essential oil, pot-pourri or incense.

Key to nature spirits

Earth spirits

Ruled by: Gnomes, ancient, dwarf-like creatures who are said to live, mainly underground or in deep forests, for a thousand years.

Rulers: Geb, or Gob, whose throne is said to be covered with crystals, silver and gold. In some wiccan traditions, the ruler of the gnomes is called Boreas, which is also the name of the Roman god of the north wind. Also Galadriel, Queen of the Earth Fairies, made famous in Tolkien's *Lord of the Rings*.

Other Earth spirits: Dark, or earth elves, gnomes, house elves, leprechauns, mine spirits, pixies, trolls (not necessarily malevolent, but very ugly), plant spirits, tree spirits and nymphs, tree mothers such as the German moss wives and *hyldermoders* in the Scandinavian and German traditions.

Earth places: Megaliths, stone circles, groves, forests, homes, temples, under hills and mountains, near ley- or psychic power lines in the earth, caves.

Animal forms they may take: Bear, bull, cat, hare or rabbit, mouse, snake, wolf.

Gifts they can bring us: Protection of ourselves and of all animals and plants; herbal and crystal wisdom, security, fertility and prosperity, realism, patience and perseverance, practical skills.

Connect with them through:

Earth crystals: Most agates, amazonite, aventurine, emerald, fossils, jet, malachite, petrified wood, rose quartz, rutilated quartz, smoky quartz, tiger's eye, all stones with holes in the centre.

Earth substances and materials: Salt, soil, herbs, flowers, trees, coins, milk, beer, honey, fruit, nuts and seeds, pot-pourri, pot plants, earth, soil or grass, forest- or animal-call music, anything green or brown.

Fragrances to connect with them: Cypress, fern, geranium, heather, hibiscus, honeysuckle, magnolia, oakmoss, patchouli, sagebrush, sweetgrass, vervain, vetivert.

Colours they like: Green and brown.

Air spirits

Ruled by: Sylphs, winged air spirits who live for hundreds of years and can, it is said, attain an immortal soul through good deeds. They never seem to age and are said to reside on mountain-tops. Sylphs may assume human form for short periods of time, and vary in size from as large as a human to much smaller, but are most usually seen in the wind.

Ruler: A mysterious being called Paralda, who is said to dwell on the highest mountain on Earth.

Other Air spirits: Fairies, light elves, sprites who frequently assume the form of birds; Spanish and Mexican *folletti,* who shape-shift into butterflies and travel on the wind, sometimes causing dust clouds; mountain spirits, nymphs and hill trolls.

Air places: Mountain-tops, hills, towers, the sky, pyramids, open plains, tall buildings, balconies, roof gardens, in clouds, on the wind.

Animal forms they may take: Bee, butterfly, eagle, hawk, birds of prey, moth, white dove, flocks of silvery or blue birds.

Gifts they can bring us: Clear focus, the ability to communicate clearly, concentration, versatility, healing powers, new beginnings, travel.

Connect with them through:

Air crystals: Blue lace agate, amethyst, citrine, danburite, diamond, lapis lazuli, clear crystal quartz, sapphire, sodalite, sugilite, turquoise.

Air substances and materials: Feathers, feathery grasses, ceiling mobiles, wind chimes, fragrances and fragrance sprays, open windows, clouds, mist, bird-call music.

Fragrances to connect with them: Acacia, almond, anise, benzoin, bergamot, dill, fennel, lavender, lemongrass, lemon verbena, lily of the valley, marjoram, meadowsweet, papyrus flower, peppermint, sage.

Colours they like: Yellow and grey.

Fire spirits

Ruled by: Salamanders, the legendary fire lizards, which are said to have originated in the Middle East in desert places. They are elongated, wand-like beings in the shape of flames, perhaps a foot or more in length. These are the least common nature spirits, best seen in bonfires or at sunset or as earth lights dancing in the sky. But mainly you see them in their animal or insect form. They can be seen in forest fires, and are also said to exist in volcanoes – the larger the source of fire, the greater the perceived size of the fairy. Like the chameleon, they are constantly changing and always moving, like flame itself.

Ruler: A flaming being called Din.

Other Fire spirits: Djinn, also jinn, from the hot, dry lands of the Middle East; dragons, genies and fire fairies, will-o'-the-wisps and earth lights.

Fire places: Bonfires, deserts, furnaces, hearths, volcanoes, sacred festival fires, hilltop beacons, all conflagrations, solar eclipses, sunrises and sunsets, lightning.

Animal forms they may take: Dragonflies, fireflies, stags, elk and moose, lions and tigers.

Gifts they can bring us: Creativity, originality, inspiration, breadth of vision, courage, success in any venture, passion and energy.

Connect with them through:

Fire crystals: Blood- and fire-agate, amber, bloodstone, boji stones, carnelian, desert rose, garnet, hematite, iron pyrites, jasper, lava, obsidian, ruby, topaz.

Fire substances and materials: Lights of all kinds, especially fibre optic lamps, sun catchers, crystal spheres of all kinds that reflect rainbows, essential oils, natural sunshine, rainbows, oranges and all orange fruit, sunflowers and all golden or orange flowers, music from hot lands, anything gold.

Fragrances to connect with them: Allspice, angelica, basil, bay, carnation, cedarwood, chamomile, cinnamon, cloves, copal, dragon's-blood, frankincense, heliotrope, juniper, lime, marigold, nutmeg, orange, rosemary, tangerine.

Colours they like: Gold, orange and red.

Water spirits

Ruled by: Undines, who originated, it is said, in the Aegean Sea and are said to live in coral caves under the ocean, the shores of lakes or banks of rivers or on marshlands. They shimmer with all the colours of water in sunlight and are so insubstantial they can rarely be seen, except clairvoyantly.

Ruler: A magical being called Necksa.

Other Water spirits: Lake spirits, ladies of the lake, Norwegian *fossegrim*, guardians of waterfalls and fjords who have mesmeric voices that can enchant mortals; mermaids, naga, serpent-like Indian water spirits.

Water places: Oceans, rivers, lakes, pools, sacred wells and streams, marshland, flood-plains.

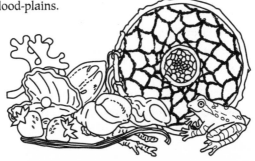

Animal forms they may take: Frogs, dolphins, whales, all fish, especially the salmon.

Gifts they can bring us: Intuition, peace, unconscious wisdom, the ability to merge and interconnect with nature in all its forms, love, abundance.

Connect with them through:

Water crystals: Aquamarine, calcite, coral, fluorite, jade, kunzite, moonstone, opal, pearl, milky quartz, selenite, tourmaline.

Water substances and materials: Milk, water, sea shells, kelp (seaweed, water features, nets or webs of any kind, dreamcatchers, fish in tanks, sea-creature and dolphin images, silk scarves, transparent drapes, silver bells on cords, anything made of silver or copper, silver foil, sea, river or dolphin music.

Fragrances to connect with them: Apple blossom, apricot, coconut, eucalyptus, feverfew, heather, hyacinth, jasmine, lemon, lemon balm, lilac, lily, myrrh, orchid, passionflower, peach, strawberry, sweet pea, thyme, valerian, vanilla, violet.

Colours they like: Blue and silver.

Nature devas

The term *deva* in Sanskrit means 'shining one'. Devas or *adhibautas* represent the higher forms of nature essences, akin to angels, the opalescent beings who watch and direct the natural world (see page 116). Some act as sacred guardians at ancient sites and of the land.

Devas have been described as golden or silver pillars of light in the morning in the clearing of a forest, or huge brown shadows near ancient circles as dusk draws in. In the Icelandic and Scandinavian traditions that spread to other parts of northern Europe including Britain, the land wights or *landvaeitir* acted as guardians of villages and settlements, passing along the fairy paths at dusk and enclosing the area in their protection. Tributes are still left to them in Iceland.

Channelling wisdom from the devas of nature

If you want to receive wisdom from one of the nature devas you will need to be patient because, though they will channel wisdom, they are not like a spirit guide, who becomes attached to one person. Their prime function is not giving humans wisdom, but overseeing the creative and destructive cycles of nature. However, in recent years much more devic communication has been reported, perhaps because they feel that humans need guidance if the planet is not to be ruined and life destroyed by global warming, pollution and deforestation.

Devic communication is less specific than the messages from nature spirits and they won't advise you on the health of your plants. However, they may inspire you if you are undertaking a major gardening project, for example when I had to rebuild my garden from builders' rubble after subsidence repairs. They will also help if you are worried about ecological issues, perhaps about the effects that nuclear waste being pumped into the oceans, oil spillages or climate change will have on future generations.

But most of all they will talk to us about patterns, about our own connection with the seasons and the ebbs and flows of the moon and the tides and with the circulation of the life-force. The devas can teach your small but essential place in the natural scheme and tell you of your personal blueprint. This can help you to reprioritise and clarify a lot of personal issues.

Talking to the devas

Very recently I have introduced much more spontaneous methods into work with nature devas to create a natural form of meditation. Try the following method, which applies as well to contacting devas at old sites as in beautiful gardens.

Choose your place with care, whether it is a flowerbed in a botanical garden, a natural circle in a forest, an old stone circle or a viewpoint among the mountains. It should be in a beautiful setting where there is also natural sound, the lapping of water, wind through trees, a waterfall or birdsong.

You may come across the spot quite by chance on a local walk, a day out or a weekend away. But as you stop there you will be flooded by a sense of the sacred and of timelessness, even if your chosen flowerbed is in a new part of a city. For all land is old and every place is filled with the experiences of all who have walked over it or lived there (see also Chapter 7).

Finally, you need light fragrance, whether pure, tangy forest air, the scent of flowers and greenery or the salt of the seas, to complete the sensory backdrop.

Morning time when it is warm is ideal; even a few minutes of warm winter sunshine may be enough – or wrap up warm on a bright, cool day.

□ Sit or half-lie propped comfortably against an old stone or a grassy mound.

□ Focus softly with half-closed eyes, first on your vista of beauty.

□ Then, still looking at the image before you, concentrate on the sounds as though turning up the volume.

□ Then move on to the fragrance, imagining it increasing in intensity.

□ Repeat the three foci in a continuous cycle: the view, the sounds and then the fragrances again, and so on.

❑ Look and listen and inhale, look, listen and inhale; keep moving from one to the other rhythmically until you start to feel sleepy and relaxed.

❑ Then create a well of silence in your mind by allowing everything, even the view, the sounds and the fragrance to merge into the background and fade.

❑ At this point you may be aware of what feels like a warm shaft of sudden, bright sunlight, a feeling of peace and utter connection with everything.

❑ You may hear words, slow and soft, as though on the breeze, or deep and measured, like thunder within the earth. Let them form and flow. Just listen and allow the words to wash over and through you. Slowly the sun will seem to fade and the scene, sounds and fragrances return.

❑ You may be left just with a single message or a deep understanding of some issue, or a great deal of information. Each experience varies.

❑ Sit for a while and then take out a notebook and scribble whatever you can recall. Some will be buried deep to emerge in dreams.

❑ You will feel a sudden breeze or chill, which is your signal to leave.

❑ Thank the guardian and leave a crystal or flower as an offering.

You probably won't know the identity of your deva, as nature devas don't have personalities in terms we can understand. However, if you return to the place, you may become aware almost at once of a pillar of light or a huge, brown shadow around the tallest stone, and know your deva is waiting.

You can also visit other places to connect with devas, but do not seek devic wisdom more than one a month. Any insights are a privilege and a gift, so don't out wear your welcome.

Animal messengers

From the earliest times, humans have revered the wisdom and qualities of animals and birds. In indigenous societies such as the Inuit and Sámi reindeer people of the Far North, animals that are hunted are treated with reverence. The entrails or bones are left at or returned to the site of the kill so that the animal spirit might be reborn. The 21st-century hunter in Scandinavia or Russia, with his mobile phone strapped to his belt, who leaves the entrails of the slain animal on a stone, is following an ancient thanksgiving ritual dating back many thousands of years.

We know from numerous accounts of the altruism of pets that animals have souls. Certainly there are on the spirit plane wise, evolved animals who act as guides to humans, perhaps appearing in the form of an actual animal or in dreams and meditation. These spirit animals are the power creatures that appeared in the form of a particularly beautiful bird or finely marked animal to Native North Americans and Australian Aboriginals on vision quests. Vision quests are spiritual journeys into the wilderness undertaken at the gateway of adulthood and at intervals during adult life.

Those creatures that appeared to people destined to become a chief, or a medicine man or woman, would reveal telepathically that they were the clan chief of their particular animal species and would reveal an important message mind to mind, sometimes for the individual to deliver to his people. These animal clan leaders might give their name and act as the totem or power animals for individuals or the whole tribe.

An individual would, on adulthood, assume the name of an animal or bird that was spiritually significant on their first vision quest, for example Running Elk.

You too may decide to adopt a secret animal or bird who seems to be your special guide and protector. You can recite its name in your mind to summon strength or focus at work or in challenging situations, for example: 'I am Golden Eagle and soar high.'

In this section I will focus on how you can identify your special creature and obtain wisdom from animal guides, both through telepathic communication with actual creatures and from discovering your own archetypal or ideal symbolic animal spirit guide that you can visualise.

Finding a living animal spirit guide

You may have always loved tigers and collected pictures, models and information about your favourite species. You may have dreamed about them, not with fear but as a symbol of protection and your own hidden strength. Then one day in a conservation park you may become fascinated by a particular tiger, whose eyes suddenly meet yours. He or she may approach the edge of the enclosure and remain quite motionless and you may sense an overwhelming connection with the creature.

Often this creature is the alter ego to your true nature. If you are gentle and quiet your tiger will encourage you to be brave, to strive for what you want and not to shrink back when you meet opposition. Over time you may adopt other animal icons as different needs emerge and your lifestyle changes, but usually your special spirit creature remains.

Though the Ancient Egyptians revered all the creatures connected with their favourite deity, for example cats in association with the cat-headed goddess Bastet, certain creatures were treated specially and buried with great ceremony. These were the ones believed to contain the spirit or special essence of the deity. So too, although all tigers, for example, might be your power creatures, one day you will see one in actuality and, through it, know your personal animal spirit guide.

Communicating with your personal animal helpers

Using cards

Some people use a commercial divinatory animal card pack, usually from the Native American, Ancient Egyptian or Celtic worlds, where the concept of animal guides is strong. This can be a way of identifying not only your root power animal, but also the different animal strengths you need in different situations.

By picking one card (or, some traditions say, two) unconsciously from a new, face-down shuffled pack, you may identify a creature who offers you special strength. If you feel no affinity with the animal card you have chosen, put it aside and the meaning may become clear later. But continue to choose until you feel the connection in your heart, whatever the instructions on the pack say.

You can also use children's animal picture cards or a selection of animal or bird postcards. Just shuffle the cards, set them in a circle face-down and turn over the one you are drawn to instinctively.

Or use your pendulum, with either a formal or home-made pack, and ask it to pull down over your correct spirit-guide anima.

Working with actual animals to discover your spirit guide

If you already have a love of a particular species, don't bother with a pack of cards.

You could also use this method if you are undecided between a number of similar species, for example a hawk or an eagle, as your power creature.

Visit different conservancies, if necessary using a holiday to another country to find the individual creature that will make the spiritual connection perhaps started in your dreams or loved from fairy tales.

Your totem may be an animal or bird indigenous to your region or one from another part of the world that attracts you. If you explore your ancestry, you can often trace the roots of your fascination to a creature from an area your forebears occupied. If your special creature lives on the other side of the world, a little detective work will often reveal that your creature may have been one indigenous to your home region hundreds or thousands of years earlier and you have tapped into the folk-memory of the place.

This all happens so spontaneously. You may look at a beloved species and feel great warmth and pleasure. Then suddenly, when you least expect it, there will be your creature. You will always love the species, but that one creature will for all times be in your heart, because he or she carries your animal spirit guide. Your eyes will meet and the connection in your mind is made in your heart. Try to obtain a picture of your special creature that you can set on your bedroom wall, use as a screen saver on your computer or carry with you, or a small charm of the creature to keep in a wallet for when you need strength.

If possible, when you meet your special creature, try to spend time at intervals during the day watching it at rest, feeding or bounding across the earth. If the animal or bird has less-than-ideal conditions then it will be an incentive for you to work for the species to improve the chances of survival for those who can return to the wild. At least you can try to improve conditions for those bred in captivity or perhaps injured in the wild.

On the other hand, your power animal may be totally accessible – a blackbird that comes into the garden or a beautiful, mystical stray cat who adopts you – and you can then enjoy regular actual contact with your personal animal spirit guide through the flesh-and-blood creature.

You also may meet others of the same species who have a message for you from your personal animal guide. They may appear in unexpected settings at a time you need reassurance – a blackbird who comes and sits motionless next to you on a bench in a city square while you are waiting for an interview or a rabbit that appears in your garden at a major crisis or change point and stays till the crisis is over. Just sit or stand quietly and enjoy the experience.

Working with your animal or bird spirit guide

Even if you do regularly see your power creature, working with the inner spirit animal is a good way of opening yourself to deeper and more prolonged wisdom from the idealised or archetypal power creature. For the imagined creature is not only a symbol of the wisest and most magnificent of the species through the ages, but also carries the accumulated wisdom of all who have worked with the same power image as yours though the ages and in different cultures. This is possible because of our shared cultural heritage and through the cosmic bank of wisdom from which we can all draw through symbols.

Find out all you can about your special creature, from books, videos, lectures and, if you are lucky, hands-on experience. A number of conservation parks and forest conservancies organise meet-the-animal days or offer the opportunity to go on a night-time bat- or owl-watching walk. Read also the myths and old stories, especially from the Native North American and Australian Aboriginal traditions, where wise creatures were instrumental in the creation of the world.

❏ Light a candle and sit facing it quietly at a time when your chosen creature would come to rest.

❏ Hold out your hands as though you were touching the creature in front of you.

❏ In your mind create its total persona, using your senses, the animal- or bird-call, the heat of its breath, the softness of its fur, the pungency of its skin.

❏ Breathe along with the visualised creature, whether panting or a soft flutter, and picture your heart beating in time with that of the creature.

❏ Now picture the creature moving closer until the two of you merge and you are seeing the world through its eyes, walking through the jungle, brushing against plants, hiding or swooping down. At this point the message will come in words, pictures or just sensations.

❏ When you are ready, move slowly away and, before you separate, touch the soft fur or feathers in your mind once more.

❏ Sit quietly and, when you are ready, record the experience in words or pictures. The message may be simple or profound.

Spend time reading stories about the animal or watching a wildlife video until you are ready to leave your power creature. He or she may come to you in sleep with more insights.

Carry out the exercise weekly or when you need wisdom from your power creature. In time you will have only to close your eyes or sit quietly in candlelight looking into the flame to call your creature and receive the necessary message.

7

Guidance from those who are no longer with us and our wise ancestors

One of the most common experiences I receive letters or e-mails about is contact with deceased relatives. Such contact may come in the form of dreams or in a sign, for example a radio suddenly changing station just in time to hear a shared song on the anniversary of a death. There may be an overwhelming sense of peace, a gentle touch, words that come into your mind, perhaps a shared joke, and you sense once more the loving presence. You may smell the favourite fragrance of your departed relative at a time when you are feeling sad, even though there is no actual perfume in the room. Some people even see or are able to touch the relative momentarily and feel not an insubstantial form, but one that is warm, vital and always young and fit, because the departed relative now appears in their inner spirit, or etheric, body, which I talked of in Chapter 5.

Children not only regularly see deceased family members but may also describe in detail a former resident of their home or someone who lived on land the family house is built on. If you are interested in learning more about this topic I have written a book called *The Psychic Power of Children* (Foulsham/Quantum), which contains many true and verified accounts of how love seems able to survive death.

Sometimes a wise relative who guided and protected us in life continues the role in the afterlife. Grandmothers and mothers, especially, keep an eye on living family members and may send a sign or appear in a dream to offer reassurance and advice.

One remarkable example I came across was the story of Sue, whose mother had died from alcohol poisoning when Sue was a young teenager. Sue had cared for her mother throughout her childhood and the death was incredibly traumatic. But death was not the end. Sue wrote to me:

'Some years later I began to see my mother in my dreams at night. These were rather more than ordinary dreams. They were completely ordered, sensible and logical. I would wake from them feeling completely satisfied, knowing that the two of us had spent hours together, simply talking things through.

'Strangely, on waking I would never remember the exact words that had been spoken, but I could remember my anger with her, her apologies and explanations, the memories we would share, the hugging. It was as if she had been sitting on my bed, just chatting.

'In 1995 my partner and I were staying with friends in Slovakia and I had been feeling out of sorts for some months with a constant pain between my shoulder blades. Fidelma, our hostess and my former yoga teacher, suggested that she should give me some reflexology. During the session I went into my usual state of deep relaxation in the candlelit room. As she worked on my feet, Fidelma told me that she was being told to give me messages and she proceeded to repeat them to me. To all intents and purposes they were meaningless, words such as "wellington boots", "the colour green – you'll know it has some special meaning", "a door in some woods".

'At this point, lying with my eyes closed I began to feel a presence on my left shoulder. My shoulder felt very warm, as if someone was standing very close to me. Fidelma suddenly said: "Sue, there is someone with you now. Do you know who it is?"

'I knew before she had finished speaking that it was my mother. I was flooded with a feeling of love for my mother, as if I was seeing a long lost friend. It was the first time my mother had managed to contact me in consciousness. All the apparently meaningless key words my mother had given me, via Fidelma, had particular significance for my mother and me.

'When the session was over, Fidelma sat with me and told me that I had reached an important moment in my life, that I had been given the power to heal other people and that I was ready to use it. I said that I did not know how. Fidelma reassured me that I would be shown. The strong implication was that my mother was now my guardian angel.

'In the very first healing class I attended, I was nervous that I would not find the ability which others believed I had. My mind was very quickly set at rest when my mother put her hand on my left shoulder and filled me with an energy the like of which I had never felt before. At that point, I realised she was making amends for the misery and lost years that we had both endured as I was growing up. It is my mother who has awakened my ability to heal and she renews my confidence whenever I doubt my ability.

'My mother and I have now become firm friends. Now it is she who guides me, not the other way round, just as it should have been all those years ago.'

Contacting those who are no longer with us

Our relatives live on the Rainbow plane, which we can access through the third, Mental layer of our aura. From numerous descriptions given by deceased relatives it would seem that on this plane in our spirit bodies we can create from our thoughts our own heaven, whether a little wooden house in the pine woods or a city apartment overlooking a glittering town. It would also seem we keep our earthly personalities intact, which is why some people still do not find happiness.

Near-death experiences reveal glimpses of an afterlife with beautiful gardens, crystal fountains, pathways of fragrant flowers and wonderful music; usually a loving relative is waiting to greet the person who momentarily dies and to send them back to life if it is not yet their time to pass over.

Wise teachers and guides on this Rainbow plane work to help even the most negative and foolish people who have died to find a positive life and perhaps help them to return to Earth to learn lessons in another body.

Fiery pits of hell were created by churchmen in different religions to keep the flock in order. Love and positive reparation for evil-doers to put right their harm and to face their wrongdoings is what the afterlife, called 'the Summerland' in spiritualism, is about. Those spirits who will not be helped wander in the darkness of their own creation – and are the ones your doorkeeper shuts out when you work with spirit guides.

Family spirit guides

Some people when they die are naturally wise and so can be helped to work as personal guides to future generations of their own family. This is why a young child may from their early days talk about and describe a deceased grandparent or great-grandparent who regularly visits them, even if they never knew the person in life or have never seen a photograph.

So great is the power of love that loving, deceased relatives can make their presence known to earthly relatives in times of need and this love will open the aura of the living person so that there can be communication.

Of course, your relatives are not always watching you – they have their own evolution to work on. But just as in life your mother will ring out of the blue to ask what is wrong, even if you have not heard from her for a while, so when we are sad or in trouble our deceased relatives will know and try to send reassurance in a way that will not frighten us. Your deceased relative will not appear before you if you would hate that or be scared, but you might smell their perfume or be aware that they are near.

How to talk to a loved relative

I get a lot of letters from people who would love to receive a sign that a parent who has died is well and happy in the afterlife and still watches over them. This can be especially important if the death was sudden or not peaceful, or there is unfinished emotional business between the two people. Others, who did get the chance to say goodbye, still wonder why they have not even dreamed about their loved one in the months after the bereavement.

There are many reasons. For some people the grief of the loss is so great the mind just could not cope and it may be two or three years before positive dreams begin. I could not even speak my mother's name for two years after her death.

The deceased person may take a while to settle into the spirit world before having the energy to contact their relatives on Earth. They may need to rest and recover, especially if the last illness was prolonged or the death was the result of an accident. You can be sure your deceased family member is being cared for by their spirit guides and other relatives who are already in the afterlife. Time is very different there and what may seem a few minutes in the afterlife may be years in Earth time.

But if you want a sign, there are ways you can make contact. Let me tell you about Zoë, whose mother had died traumatically. Zoë had felt quite unreasonably guilty that she had not been with her mother in her last moments and had waited for two years for a sign from her mother.

Zoë and I worked together during one of the private sessions I hold in the UK and Sweden. Zoë dropped the healing herb rosemary into a pink candle-flame and spoke in her mind what she wanted to say to her mother in those last moments. Then she blew out the candle.

Instantly the smoke went horizontally towards Zoë and split, curling around Zoë's head and shoulders as though hugging her. Then it disappeared. Zoë felt her mother with her.

After Zoë had gone I relit the candle several times, but the smoke would not do that again.

If there is a particular deceased relative you would like to contact, work on their birthday or a day that was special to both of you.

❏ Choose a small memento, perhaps a gift from them or an item bought on a shared holiday that evokes happy or humorous memories.

- ❏ Go to a favourite place in your garden or a local park or square, taking the memento with you.

- ❏ Sit quietly in the place and let happy memories, conversations and jokes flow through your mind.

- ❏ Recall the familiar voice and any fragrances – wood smoke, tobacco, aftershave, perfume or soap – that remind you of your relative.

- ❏ When you are ready, go indoors and, even if it is not dark, light a rose- or lavender-scented candle.

- ❏ Look into the flame and speak your words of love and any of regret. When you have finished, blow out the candle and let the light be a link of love with the essential person who lives on in the afterlife and also in their descendants (including you), and in all the kind deeds they performed and wise words they spoke during life.

You may be rewarded with a sense of peace, perhaps a fleeting shadow, and a touch light as gossamer, words softly spoken in the once-familiar voice in your mind's ear or externally. You may smell momentarily the fragrance associated with the loved one.

Your relative would not appear if this would trouble or frighten you, and you are not summoning spirits. Even if you do not believe in the afterlife, you can connect with the essential love that never dies.

Continuing the connection

Begin a memory box in a small wooden or metal container. Start it with the memento you used to make the first connection.

Over the weeks, add mementoes of your loved one, a favourite item of jewellery, a medal, a school or trades certificate, a letter sent to you, poems or sketches he or she made, photographs of your loved one's life, a holiday postcard, a travel card or passport, a pressed dried flower from their wedding bouquet or buttonhole, a button from a favourite coat or any newspaper cuttings in which he or she featured.

Add a small sachet or purse of lavender or rose petals fragranced on the outside with a favourite perfume, cologne or aftershave. You can renew the sachet when the fragrance fades.

- ❏ When you need advice from your deceased relative, open the box and hold any treasure you wish.

- ❏ Ask about something that troubles you or on which you would benefit from their opinion.

❏ Wait, but if the answer does not come into your mind, light a white candle next to the item and the open box. You may like to spend time looking through the box as the candle burns through.

❏ When the candle has gone out, close the box, but place the chosen item close to your bed.

You may dream of your relative and even see their home in the afterlife. Alternatively, a sign may come the following day to answer the question, often as a tune you hear that you both liked, and whose words contain a message – or the answer may come as a familiar catchphrase they used that pops into your mind.

Mediumship

Mediumship is the process in which a sensitive person, called a 'medium', or 'channel', is used by spirits to communicate with the living, and by living relatives to ask, via the medium, questions of the spirits.

Your spirit guide may occasionally show you in your mind a deceased relative of the friend or colleague with whom you are speaking. You may or may not see the figure externally at the living person's side. The appearance of this presence will occur because there is a message you need to transmit to the living relative or because their deceased relative knows your friend or colleague needs earthly reassurance.

Choose a quiet time and by tactfully steering the conversation, you may discover that it is an anniversary of the death of the apparition you saw, or that the living person has a problem.

You may be given guidance for them via your spirit guide from the deceased relative who contacted you on their behalf.

If your friend seems happy to talk of the relative (you will have to be clever to move the conversation to the topic) you can ask what the relative would have advised in the particular dilemma had they been alive.

You may see details of the face in your mind's eye, or a distinctive garment or piece of jewellery, and so be able to hint that your friend or acquaintance is protected by a loving relative and that the person remains close.

But tread as if on eggshells. Some people may want to know what you can see and hear and gain comfort from it. Others get incredibly spooked at the idea of a deceased relative over their shoulder and, if you force their spiritual development or tell them about the ghost, they can become distressed or afraid.

As you evolve spiritually, these mediumistic experiences may occur more frequently. You may even see the spirit guides of other people (they will usually be much mistier, as they are on a higher spiritual level than the presences who are relatives). But go very slowly and cautiously. If you want to develop mediumistic powers formally, where you act as a channel for the deceased relatives and guides of other people, perhaps in a professional capacity, take training either through a Spiritualist Church or a healing organisation.

Teaching you the art is beyond the scope of this book, as you really do need to develop slowly and with support so you don't get in a mess psychologically and psychically. Even the wisest spirit guide, your doorkeeper and guardian angel will have trouble protecting you if you rush in rescuing wandering spirits, calling up deceased relatives for other people, using ouija boards and transmitting messages to everyone you meet, no matter how much light you surround yourself with.

Ask your spirit guide to help you find a reputable organisation, because this is an area you need earthly help to develop, but it can be incredibly worthwhile.

Encountering your wise ancestors

There may already be a member of your family who died, perhaps many years before you were born, but to whom through family stories you feel particularly close spiritually. Perhaps they followed a similar life path. Alternatively, you may focus on a family hero or heroine who, hundreds of years ago, brought the family from the countryside to find work in the city, or across an ocean, or who was a sailor, a missionary or a wise healer. He or she may just be waiting for you to express willingness to be guided by them. No doubt they are already in the background.

You can ask your spirit guide to confirm that you have chosen the correct character from the family past or if there is another family member who already watches over you. Once you have the name, try to write down all you know about them and allow your pen to create a story about unknown aspects of their life. Visit museums and read about the world they lived in.

A good time to make the initial connection is one of the transitions of the year – New Year's Eve, Halloween, May Eve or one of the Sun festivals, such as the longest or shortest day (around 21 June and 21 December respectively) or the equinoxes (around 21 March and 22–23 September).

❏   Sit close to an open window as night falls and place a protective clove of garlic on each of the inner window ledges of the room.

❏   Sprinkle salt along the inner window ledges and along the inner thresholds of any doors in the room, saying:

> *Welcome all who come in love and peace. I ask protection of my guide, my angel and the wise doorkeeper on this, my spiritual journey.*

☐ Leave the doors closed.

☐ Light a white candle where the breeze will cause it to flicker but not go out. Say:

> *May Great-grandfather William, who built his own house in a forest clearing to escape from persecution, guide me on my life path, if it is right to be.*

☐ Watch the moving candle-flame and you may sense a benign presence and see in your mind a scene from the life of your chosen family guide.

☐ When the scene fades, ask softly:

> *Do you have a message for me?*

☐ Wait. You may hear in your mind a different voice from that of your spirit guide and angel. Alternatively, your own inner voice may transmit a few words from the ancestor or you may see a second scene that clarifies an issue for you in your present life.

☐ This first encounter is usually brief, and when you sense the presence fading, say softly:

> *I thank you all, wise guardians and especially you, Great-grandfather William, for agreeing to my request. Come to me in my dreams and when I call you, if the time is right for you. And so depart in peace with my blessings.*

☐ Make a pledge to yourself to revive an old family custom or do more for family togetherness, even if you have difficult living relatives.

☐ Close the windows and clear away the salt, dissolving it in running water.

☐ Bury the garlic to the west of your home, the direction of the wise ancestors.

Finding your spiritual ancestor guide

For many of us there is a missing link, even if we feel very close to our blood family. You may, for example, feel far more connected with your roots when you are in the tombs of Ancient Egypt, on the mountains in Spain or looking over an industrial landscape half-way across the world from your home. You cannot explain the link genealogically, and yet the peace or joy you experience may momentarily seem more real than the life to which you return.

Often this experience is linked to a past life, perhaps that of an ancestor so far back the connection could not be proved. Some believe it may reside in a past world that you experienced yourself and which had such deep significance it has remained buried in your consciousness.

If you already know the place that is your spiritual home, try to visit the area and stay in a hotel or at a camping ground as close to you can to the spot where the feeling was strongest. Spend time quietly there, not attempting to evoke memories, but allowing the sounds, the fragrances and the colours of the present scene to form a kaleidoscope within that may re-form into momentary patchworks of other times.

While on holiday you may dream of a particular person connected with the place, and an unexpected turn in the road the next day may show you the place of your dreams. Here, if you sit and wait, your spiritual ancestor guardian who is rooted in this particular spot will come to you and the connection will be complete. You have come home.

You may be walking round a museum, a reconstructed historic dwelling or a ruined temple or abbey and find a picture or sculpture of your physical double or someone with whom you sense instant kinship.

I found my Egyptian alter ego in Cairo Museum in a brightly painted statue of a scribe's wife with whom I felt an instant spiritual link. Hossam, my guide, commented how much she resembled me physically. I use her image in my mind to connect me when I feel alienated spiritually. She often comes to me in dreams and in quiet daytime moments with her calm but always accurate wisdom.

You will find that your spiritual ancestor guardian does help you on your spiritual journey, perhaps explaining why you were drawn to a wise teacher from a particular culture (see page 56) and helping you to explore your own past connections with ancient cultures.

Creating a doorway to meet your spiritual ancestor

If you have not encountered your spiritual ancestor guardian and would like to, use the doorway technique. However, you should not feel pressurised to work with this or any other spirit guide unless you want to. There may be other priorities in your life right now.

You can use either an amethyst geode – a hollowed-out rock formation filled with tiny amethyst crystals or an oval mirror set on a table and propped against a wall. Work in the evening, sitting at a table.

❑ If using a mirror, set candles on raised surfaces behind where you will be sitting so that their light reflects in the glass.

❑ You can, if you wish, experiment with positioning the candles so that their reflections appear as a pathway at the back of the mirror.

❑ Light the candles and extinguish all other lights.

❑ Now draw a doorway in the mirror using either a washable gold or black marker, or lipstick. The doorway should be large enough to frame your head and shoulders as you sit in front of the mirror.

❑ Alternatively, set your geode on a table in front of you and arrange tea lights so that they shine into the centre of the geode and create a doorway. Again you can position other candles to shine in the darkness and create light round the geode.

❑ Look through the open doorway and in the far distance picture a small figure that moves closer and closer.

❑ Clear your mind of expectations and focus on the lights in or around the doorway, looking through half-closed eyes so that they blur slightly.

❑ Allow the figure to build up until it is framed by the doorway on the other side from you and you can see the world from which he or she has come. You may sense immediate kinship even though the figure may not be the one you were consciously expecting. But afterwards you will realise your spiritual ancestor could have been no other, and the presence will help you to understand all kinds of half-finished dreams and affinities in your life.

❑ For now, just smile and the figure will smile back.

Then you will have an overwhelming desire to close your eyes and when you open them after a minute or two, the figure will be gone.

You can repeat this exercise whenever you wish, and each time the guide will stay longer and show you more of the world from which he or she comes. If using a mirror, clean and polish the glass and redraw the doorway each time. For the geodes use fresh tea lights.

When you feel ready, you may step through the doorway knowing your spiritual ancestor will care for you and bring you back when the time is right. Your guide may talk to you of his or her world and show you their life. You can ask questions, the answer to which will appear in your mind or in a place you are drawn to visit over the following days.

Add to your knowledge of your spiritual ancestor's world and you will visit it in dreams that seem more than dreams (see page 129) and in quiet daytime moments. The experience is yours and your guide's to use as you will.

At the end, when you return to the doorway on your side, turn and say goodbye. Always close your eyes to allow your spiritual ancestor to leave by his or her own route, which you are not permitted to see. Nothing bad will happen if you do look, but you will probably just see mist, and your guide may be less willing to work with you for a while.

Making the place of the ancestors

The Ancient Egyptians had special altars in their temples where offerings could be left for the wise ancestors; each family tomb of the wealthy had its offerings place.

The Romans also had their offerings table for family ancestors in their homes. The lares were the Roman deified ancestors or heroes and the *lar familiaris* was the spirit of the founder of the house, who never left it. In many cultures, at festival times the ancestors are still welcomed to the family hearth.

If you have room in your home, you could create a table for the ancestors. This is a good way of showing children that death is just a natural phase on our longer journey and of helping other people to be less afraid of what we call 'ghosts' but who are in fact those who lived and loved, were part of a family, and still are.

Set a small side table against any west-facing wall. West is the direction of the ancestors. Have photographs of family members who are no longer with you, small family treasures and a vase of white flowers on the table. Make the table your own and perhaps encourage family members to find symbols or photographs of loved, deceased family members.

You can also keep here any memory boxes, plus symbols of the worlds of your personal family ancestor and your spiritual ancestor. You could perhaps find a small book of photographs of the time your chosen physical ancestor lived, as well as images of the perhaps more exotic world of your spiritual ancestor. For example, if he or she is an Ancient Egyptian, you might choose a small crystal pyramid or a statue of one of the deities in whose temple he or she worshipped.

Set an offerings dish on the table. Make the offerings quite personal when you are recalling a known ancestor, for example a beloved grandmother's favourite perfume in a small bottle, or a few of her favourite chocolates or flowers. Give the chocolates to children or visitors to spread the joy. For ancestors more distant in time and spiritual kin, offer incense, small fruits, crystals or dried flowers in the bowl. Keep the offerings fresh and change them every few days, stopping to touch the focal symbol of your ancestors and allowing wise words to come into your mind.

On any special anniversaries, light a candle and perhaps share the jokes, holiday photos and stories of the deceased kin with other family members and cook their favourite foods to share at a family meal.

8

Working with archangels, saints and ascended beings

Reassessing the path of spirit

Now our journey goes upwards in spiritual terms. Let's assess the path so far. First we worked with your personal spirit guide, the most important and ever-present guide in your life. Here you became aware of the doorkeeper, who offers protection from negative spirit forces. Then you encountered helper guides: the life teacher guide, who assists with practical learning of tasks and skills and the spirit physician, who oversees our health.

After that we graduated to senior spirit school and explored the world of our guardian angel and those higher teachers who come from wise traditions and help us to explore healing and increase our spiritual growth. We left this path briefly in Chapter 5 to expand the background to the different planes on which various guides operate. Then we visited the planes of the nature spirits and our own deceased family members and wise ancestors to meet the individual guides who would work best with us.

The fifth plane, the realm of the higher beings

As we become adjusted to working with spirit guides on all these different levels and planes, so our spiritual horizons continue to expand. This means we are able to bring into play the higher levels of our own spiritual energies that are present in our aura, or psychic-energy field, at the fifth aura level, the Etheric template. At this point we have access to the Atmic plane (see page 135).

So we can at last, whether after weeks, months or years, make connection with the plane of the archangels and highest beings, including those shining devas who oversee the blueprint of nature and co-ordinate the work of the nature devas we met in gardens and old places. On the fifth plane also are the master teachers, often geniuses who in the afterlife have chosen to develop music or literature to the highest level. Finally, here are the ascended beings, the great teachers of humanity from past times on Earth who are still willing to devote themselves to teaching humans, albeit from a higher plane.

This is where the analogy of junior school (your spirit guide, the nature spirits and the wise ancestors) ends, because this plane is a huge leap from the realm of angels and higher teachers, akin to the highest learning in the most elevated university, multiplied a million times.

Encountering higher beings

You can't, then, light a candle and expect the Archangel Michael to stop overseeing the weather and nations and organising the hierarchies of angels to look for your lost cat, or Gautama Buddha to give you private lessons in spirituality.

The Atmic plane is the level at which higher beings give wisdom to a thousand other people at the same time as you are channelling (or receiving in your mind) their wise words. We, of course, see and speak to St Michael in his complete form, not just a little bit of him. But Joe in Ohio and Mary in Sydney, as well as a host of other mortals, are also working with St Michael and seeing their version of the complete St Michael at precisely the same moment.

There are angelic paintings from different periods that you can find in books and art galleries and through your web browser if you want to see how other people pictured the archangels. There are also images and statues of the ascended beings such as the oriental goddess Kwan Yin.

However, all these depictions are based on the human mind's attempts to describe a presence that is beyond human description or human existence. So, for example, in the next section, though I have briefly suggested a common way the archangels are visualised, your own image of the four archangels will emerge and this will become for you the personalised aspect of the omnipresent archangel energy.

The key is omnipresence, which means that these higher beings can be everywhere and be seen by a lot of people at the same time. This is a concept that is also relevant on the highest plane that we can reach: the level of divinity, which I describe in the final chapter.

Because these spirit forms are beyond the strictly personal level, ritual and prayer become important tools. Ritual can not only structure our experiences, but also enable us to communicate through channels established over hundreds or even thousands of years with higher beings.

Be wary of the inevitably spiritually superior soul who informs you condescendingly she works only with the Archangel Gabriel or that a being of light with an obscure name has endowed only her with a precise description how the universe operates. This guru-in-waiting is just deciding which publisher to bless with this unique wisdom to enlighten the world – and make her fortune. Such souls are generally talking to their egos. That said, they still make me feel like the girl who put her shoes on the wrong feet, though I have yet to see their works in print.

The archangels

These are the higher angels, traditionally seven in number, who guard the throne of the God or Goddess, act as messengers for important events and may be guardians to a city or even a nation. Some confusion arises because archangels appear in other religions apart from Judaism and Christianity and their names and roles vary. There are only four archangels in Islam and ten in the Kabala, the esoteric Jewish system of spirituality. In the Authorised version of the Bible only three archangels are mentioned: Michael, Gabriel and Raphael, and so they tended to be credited with the functions of many non-biblical archangels.

For much spiritual and magical work, Uriel, who appeared in the apocryphal Book of Enoch, is included, and is the fourth traditional archangel who has passed into Western magical traditions from the Middle Ages onwards. These four have retained their importance in modern rituals (see pages 26–7).

In this chapter we will work with the four main archangels you met in Chapter 2. Each archangel rules the first hour after sunrise of his own day (see below). Though many people do regard the archangels as male, others consider them androgynous so I have called them 'he' here merely for convenience.

Dawn can be a particularly good time to contact an archangel to receive his special blessing and perhaps to receive messages in your mind.

Archangel signs

In the ancient magical writings there is an angelic script, used for writing messages to angels and archangels and in other forms of magical ritual.

Below are the four glyphs associated with the four main archangels. You can use these glyphs at the head of a blank piece of paper if you are channelling wisdom using automatic writing (see pages 59–60) or if you are writing a letter to an archangel as part of a ritual (see page 114).

You can also carve or etch the individual signs on the side of a candle you burn in a ritual, and paint the sign on a crystal and carry it in a small purse to take with you the power and protection of a particular archangel whose strength you need in your life.

Uriel, Archangel of Earth and the North

His **colour** is red.

His **planet** is Mars ♂.

His **crystals** are amber, carnelian, hematite, obsidian, rutilated quartz, tiger's eye.

His **incenses** are basil, bay, copal, ginger, rosemary, sandalwood.

His **day** is Tuesday.

His **red candle** can be inscribed with the archangel glyph shown above or with the planetary sign for Mars.

Uriel, whose name means 'Fire of God', is the archangel who brought alchemy to humankind. Alchemy is the sacred art of transmuting base metal into gold. Uriel also instructed Moses in the Kabala, the esoteric system of Hebrew spirituality and magic by which humankind could be reunited with God. Uriel guards the gates of the Garden of Eden with his fiery sword until we are ready to return to Paradise by our own efforts.

He is said to be a pure pillar of fire and so can best be invoked just before dawn to mark the transition to a day when we need to make significant efforts. He also blazes in a fiery sunset.

As Archangel of the North and the element Earth, Uriel can bring warmth to the winter season and to cold or unhappy periods in our life. He melts the snows with his flaming sword or torch.

Ask Uriel for protection, for change of all kinds, for the fulfilment of a long-term spiritual path, for quelling anger in others and transforming our own powerful emotions, such as fury, jealousy, resentment and spite into impetus for positive change; also for focusing ourselves single-mindedly on making the world a better and safer place.

Spiritually Uriel will inspire us to work with angels, devas and higher spiritual essences, to perfect our vision of divine realms and refine our spiritual nature by burning away our deep-seated desire for comfort and acceptance of the status quo.

Visualise him in rich, burnished gold and ruby-red with the brightest flame-like halo, like a bonfire blazing in the darkness, holding his fiery sword.

Raphael, Archangel of Air and the East

His **colour** is yellow.

His **planet** is Mercury, the winged messenger ☿.

His **crystals** are golden beryl, yellow calcite, citrine and yellow jasper.

His **incenses** are fennel, fern, lavender, mint, pine and thyme.

His **day** is Wednesday.

His **yellow candle** can be inscribed with the archangel glyph shown above or with the planetary sign for Mercury.

Raphael, whose name means 'God heals', is the healer archangel and travellers' guide. He is the angel who offers healing to the planet and to mankind and all creatures on the face of the Earth and in the skies and waters. He is also guardian of the young. He is depicted with a pilgrim's stick, a wallet and a fish, showing the way and offering sustenance to all who ask.

As Archangel of Air and the East he can waken the spring in our hearts at any time and cause new growth, both in spring and when it is needed.

Ask Raphael for healing of all kinds and to fight against technological and chemical pollution and the adverse effects of modern living, to help us make change and to start again, for optimism and clarity of thought, also to protect children and animals and anyone who is lost physically or emotionally.

Spiritually Raphael will alleviate the worries of daily lives that keep us bound to the Earth, and show us how to teach others our spiritual insights; he will awaken our higher healing powers.

Visualise him in the colours of early-morning sunlight, with a beautiful, green healing ray emanating from his halo.

Michael, Archangel of Fire and the South

His **colour** is gold.

His **planet** is the Sun ☉.

His **crystals** are amber, carnelian, clear quartz crystal and golden topaz.

His **incenses** are chamomile, frankincense, marigold, rosemary and sage.

His **day** is Sunday.

His **gold candle** can be inscribed with the archangel glyph shown above or with the planetary sign for the Sun.

Sometimes called the Archangel of the Sun, Michael is the Archangel of Light and is the warrior angel. He appeared to Moses as the fire in the burning bush, and saved Daniel from the lions' den. As commander of the heavenly hosts, Michael, who is usually pictured with a golden sword, drove Satan and his fallen angels out of the celestial realms; as Angel of Judgement he also carries a scale weighing the souls of the dead. According to the Koran, the cherubim were created from Michael's tears.

As Archangel of Fire and the South Michael is the angel of power and of illumination and brings in the summer season and growth and energy into our lives.

Ask Michael for the power to overcome any obstacles, for wisdom, illumination and also direction to the right path, for all creative ventures and for original ideas, for developing our unique gifts, for reviving barren land despoiled by industrialisation, and for cleansing air pollution.

Spiritually Michael is the archangel who opens the door to connection with the divinity and who will act as guide to the higher planes.

Visualise him resplendent in scarlet and gold with a huge sword in one hand, golden scales in his other and often a dragon crushed beneath his feet.

Gabriel, Archangel of Water and the West

His **colour** is silver.

His **planet** is the Moon ☽.

His **crystals** are moonstone, opals, pearls, milky quartz and selenite.

His **incenses** are jasmine, lilac, mimosa, myrrh and rose.

His **day** is Monday.

His **silver candle** can be inscribed with the archangel glyph shown above or with the planetary sign of the Moon.

Gabriel appears many times in the Bible, visiting the Virgin Mary and her cousin Elizabeth, mother of John the Baptist, to tell them that they were to bear sons who would lead mankind to salvation. It was Gabriel who parted the waters of the Red Sea so that the Hebrews could escape from the Pharaoh's soldiers.

Gabriel is usually pictured holding a sceptre or a lily. To the followers of Islam, Gabriel is the Spirit of Truth, who dictated the Koran to Mohammed.

Because his season is autumn, Gabriel represents the fruits of the harvest, the rewards of our successes and the need to let go of our failures and regrets.

Ask Gabriel for protection against inclement weather, for safe travel across water, to take away sorrow and to diminish self-destructive tendencies. Gabriel also cleanses polluted seas, lakes and rivers.

Spiritually Gabriel brings mystical experiences, astral travel and significant dreams, especially after prayer and meditation or in a beautiful natural place close to water; he also brings deepening spirituality within the family and work environments.

Visualise him in robes of silver with the crescent moon as his halo, surrounded by silver stars.

An archangel ritual

When you have chosen your focus archangel (you can work with different archangels for different needs), adapt the following ritual. Carry out the ritual either on the day of your chosen archangel in the hour after dawn, if possible, or whenever you have a chance during that day or evening.

☐ Light your archangel candle. If you wish, inscribe it with a screwdriver or sharp nail with the appropriate symbol, either the archangel glyph or the planetary sign.

☐ Light your incense and, if you have one, set an archangel crystal in front of it.

☐ With a silver or gold ink marker pen write on a square of dark paper what is in your heart and what you might not even want to tell your best friend, mother or partner.

☐ If you wish, you can begin with the appropriate archangel glyph. Then write down any questions you have and the need you wish to be fulfilled. State what you will do in return to help others.

☐ Read the finished letter, sign it and pass the incense smoke over it in a clockwise circle nine times.

☐ Place the letter in a white envelope and seal it, writing the archangel glyph on the front.

☐ Make the archangel glyph nine times in smoke over the sealed envelope and drip a single drop of wax on the back.

☐ When the wax is cool, etch the angel glyph in it with your pin.

☐ Leave your letter in front of the candle until the incense has burned through. Blow out the candle if still alight.

☐ Place the letter in a box with a lid, on the highest shelf you have in the highest room of your house and leave it there.

Your answer may come in your dreams or in a sudden, unexpected opportunity or challenge, or it may take longer to emerge.

Each time you write an archangel letter, add it to the box. When the box is full, tie the letters with three knots with green cord and put them away with your treasures. Begin again, using the same box.

Once a year, on the anniversary of the first archangel ritual, make a special time to read your archangels letters, both those stored away and those in the box, and see how they have been answered in your life.

Burn the letters, if possible on an outdoor fire, and cleanse the box by spiralling any incense stick over it nine times anti-clockwise, then nine times clockwise.

Do not use archangel rituals more than once a month.

Working with universal light and cosmic energies

We work within the frame of our own experience and so we interpret the energies of higher powers within our own cultural context, perhaps childhood religious teachings, and later through the writings of others, including mystics, saints and philosophers throughout the ages. These writers have attempted to categorise and describe what they have felt, seen and heard in visions, dreams and altered states of consciousness.

Inevitably, because humans categorise such experiences in hierarchies, there are numerous divisions in opinions between the number and nature of different planes of experience, the names of various elevated beings and who precisely lives where.

However, you may find the divisions artificial and unnecessarily complex, and prefer to make your own contact with divine powers, working with figures from religion, mythology and history that seem to have meaning for you.

What I will do is to briefly describe some of the ways these higher powers have been visualised, and you may like to try working with these concepts or reading more about a particular topic that interests you.

The saints

Saints are those people who have performed miracles in their lifetimes and whose miraculous powers have been witnessed after their earthly death. Even people who are not strictly religious may pray to or ask the help of saints. For example, St Francis of Assisi, patron saint of animals and birds, is a popular icon for all who love, work with and heal animals or birds. It is said that St Francis, who was born in the late 1100s, established the first Christmas crib, discovered in 1223 in a cave in the hills of Grecchia, using real animals so that people could understand the true significance of Christmas.

St Jude is invoked throughout the world for matters that seem hopeless, St Anthony of Padua for finding missing people, articles or animals, and St Joseph, the father of Jesus, for all who are seeking employment.

Each country has its patron saints. If you explore churches in your region you may find saints with whom you feel special kinship and from whom you might seek guidance, or you may find your own trade or city has its own saintly patron. Lighting a candle to them and asking their help can be a good focus in your spiritual work.

Higher-plane teachers

These include those great masters and mistresses of philosophy, literature and music who did not live such bad lives that they were unable to carry their gifts with them to the afterlife because of negativity.

Ascended masters

Ascended masters are a Far Eastern concept that filtered into the West via theosophy. Indeed Madame Blavatsky, the founder of theosophy, said that the true teachers of theosophical wisdom were the mahatmas, the 'old souls', or 'masters of wisdom', as they were known in India. Although they had completed their own cycles of earthly incarnations, they returned to teach those who might understand and disseminate their message.

A number of other sages and great teachers of humanity have also been identified as masters who have ascended, sometimes, it is said, in their bodies, to higher planes and choose to guide humanity. These wise teachers have either created major systems of philosophy and religion or are close to deities. They include the Chinese sage Confucius, Jesus in his human form, the Virgin Mary, Gautama Buddha, St Germain and the Hindu Krishna, an avatar, or earthly form, of the god Vishnu, the preserver of the universe. Another is Kwan Yin, the mother goddess of compassion and abundance who passed into Tibetan philosophy (women are also called masters). But there are countless others who have spoken through dreams, meditation and sometimes art forms such as music or painting.

If you want to know more about these icons of wisdom, enter their names on your web browser or look for a book in your library. You may find a master who seems to fit in with your own concept of spirituality and then you can use the ritual on pages 117–19 to channel wisdom.

Devas

Devas in their purest form are beings, or huge columns or pyramids, of light, as big as a mountain. If you have found it helpful working with nature devas in beautiful places, you may, as you evolve spiritually, sense that beyond them is a less tangible device. These are the source of the life-force (see page 88), also called 'prana' or 'ch'i', that is filtered to us through flowers, trees and crystals.

These light beings are quite hard to work with because you have no name or identity on which to focus your visualisation of this unearthly form. These are the beings that control the star clusters and the planets, and try to stop world leaders from using weapons of mass destruction and allowing global warming to continue. But, if you do get a chance to connect with a light deva, you will feel so energised and empowered, and yet so peaceful, that it is well worth the effort and you will glow for weeks.

Channelling wisdom from a higher source

If there is a particular saint, ascended master or archangel with whom you feel affinity, focus this ritual on him or her. Before you begin, collect images and statues and read about their life and any existing recorded channelling they have given to others. Increasingly, people are publishing their experiences with higher beings on the internet.

Alternatively, focus in your mind on a huge devic pillar of light or allow your own wise guides to connect you with the source of wisdom you would most benefit from.

You can also use this method to connect with the God or Goddess forms I have described in the final chapter.

You can work in your home in your spirit-guide place or your garden. Having a bath using lavender or rose essential oil or foam would help you to get in the mood. However, the first time, try to make the occasion special, in a sacred building or outdoors in a place of beauty or an ancient sacred site. Abbey gardens are ideal. Perhaps you could pick a holiday time or a weekend away for your first channelling ritual so you have plenty of time.

Find your spot well in advance and, if it is in a sacred building, check opening times and if the building is scheduled to be used, for example, for a religious service.

Eat and drink only a little unprocessed food during the two or three hours before your ritual.

Avoid contact through phones or e-mails for three hours before and, if possible, spend the time alone letting your mind settle and empty. If you have young children or other commitments this may be difficult. So, five minutes before you start, close your eyes and picture stars in a velvet-blue sky going out one by one to settle yourself.

Work so that light is all around you, whether church candles, light through a stained-glass window, or natural sun, moon or starlight.

❑ Focus on an area of light, and from it create a pillar of light in your mind, even if you are working with a specific saint or archangel.

❑ Still looking at the physical light, allow a face and perhaps a person to form from it, if you are focusing on a particular archangel or master teacher. Use some of the images you have seen in books or pictures to get your mind started, but let your own vision take precedence.

❑ You may continue to see brilliance. This does not mean your master teacher is not present, merely that the experience is more intense than you imagined it might be.

❑ Touch your hairline or the crown of your head with your power hand, the one you write with, saying:

Above me the sky.

❑ Touch next your brow, saying:

Within me the light.

❑ Touch next your throat, saying:

To receive wisdom true.

❑ Finally, touch your heart and say:

To kindle the flame within.

❑ Next, ask that only goodness and light may enter the place and your mind.

❑ Then wait.

You may feel as though your mind is filled with radiance.

You may become aware of a vibrating or humming and perhaps flashes of different rays of colour.

There may be a voice, music, poetry or an overwhelming sense of being in the presence of your saint or master teacher.

There is usually fairly early on a sense of rightness as though you had been waiting all your life for this moment. You may hear words from the Bible, the I Ching or religious teachings, perhaps from another faith than your own.

You can ask who is speaking and you can ask questions, although channelling tends to be more effective if you listen and allow the higher form to direct the dialogue.

Often the words are secondary to the feeling of being blessed and connected to the source of light, so you should not restrict the moment with expectations or an agenda.

Gradually the brilliance will fade from your mind and the voice recede, as though down a tunnel.

❑ Thank the essence and sit quietly, allowing the vibrations to steady down.

You may feel a sense of loss, as though a beloved friend has gone away. But be reassured that the experience can be repeated and each time will be longer and easier to comprehend.

Channel this wisdom no more than once a fortnight, if possible at the same time and in the same place. You will, if you are patient, learn more about the higher energy that pours down.

Channelling wisdom from a higher source using automatic writing

You have already encountered automatic writing as a means of communicating with spirit energies. This is merely the next level up. You could take your special pen and paper wrapped in white silk in your bag and write immediately afterwards or wait till you return to your home or hotel.

Use the special pen and paper you keep for automatic writing, but before you begin, unless you are in the place where you received the wisdom, waft spirals of lavender or rose incense smoke over it.

❑ Wherever you are writing, ask the protection of your guides and angels so that you may transmit the wisdom you have experienced with truth and humility.

❑ Light pure white candles to rekindle the experience if you are away from the setting where it occurred.

❑ Wherever you are, breathe in light very slowly before beginning and softly sigh out on your out breaths any doubts or fears that have crept in.

Your personal spirit guide, who shared the experience with you but remained in the background, will help you to make connection with the words.

You may again hear the voice of the higher energy whose wisdom you are channelling.

❑ If not, let your mind go blank and the higher force will guide your hand to write the correct words.

You may find more information than you originally received, or connections will be given between what seemed unconnected ideas.

❑ When your pen slows or you feel tired, stop, as you will not receive anything else of worth today.

❑ Thank your source of wisdom and your own guide and read the words the pen has written. Even if they do not all make sense, you can copy them at a later time into your spirit journal.

Over time these communications will build up to help you to understand more of the higher planes and mysteries of the universe. In future experiences, you may wish to ask if other masters or devas will work with you but it is likely that one is especially accessible.

Before we move on to the highest levels of spiritual experience in the final chapter, I would like to suggest a method of healing friends and family using the energies you have tapped into in this chapter. If you rely on your guides and angels you do not need formal training to send healing to those you love. However, if you do want to go on to heal others more formally there are a number of healing systems you can learn through classes and books.

Channelling healing with higher energies

The method below does not belong to a specific healing tradition, though it has similarities with a number. It is one I learned from a wise old healer in the UK who has seen and worked with angels since she was quite young and which I have adapted to my own healing work.

Either work in natural daylight or supplement a dull day with white candles or soft lamps so you and the person you are healing are sitting in a pool of light. Have a bowl of mineral water ready at the end of the exercise to cleanse the crystals you used.

❑ Ask the person you are healing to choose two crystals from your special angel crystals (see page 55) or two from an amethyst, fluorite, rose quartz, jade or a very small clear quartz sphere.

❑ Let them decide which hand to hold which crystal in and ask them to open their hands flat with a crystal in each palm.

❑ Close your hands, one over each crystal so you are connecting with the patient's hands and crystals so the three energies combine.

❑ At this point you may sense or see your personal guide and guardian angel and also those of your patient. If you know the person well you could try to describe their guide and angel.

❑ Now ask for the help of Raphael, any wise teachers who have been working with you on healing and your own highest source of light, who may be another archangel, a higher deva, a saint or one of the ascended beings. Alternatively, if you prefer, just picture pure white light streaming down and ask silently for the help of whoever is right to act as your healing guide on this occasion.

❑ Ask your patient if they would prefer to sit or lie, then release their hands and ask them to hold the crystals cupped lightly in each hand.

❑ Stand at the side of the patient and make an arch with your hands over your own head.

❑ Then hold your fingers directly up to the light over your head.

❑ Visualise the angelic force or radiant light transmitting pure gold and white liquid power through the crown of your own head, down through your brow, down through the throat chakra (into your heart chakra and then upwards and outwards through your arms to your fingers (see page 73 for the chakra positions). Remember the heart controls the minor chakras in the hands. As the light enters your outstretched fingertips, you may be aware of tingling or faint golden sparks.

❑ Describe the process to the patient, who may be able to see the light or feel the warmth radiating.

❑ Transfer your hands to 2 or 3 centimetres (about an inch) above the centre of the patient's head, where the crown chakra is, so your fingers are pointing straight downwards.

❑ Begin to talk and let words flow, describing cascading golden waterfalls, gentle rivers, cool hillsides, deep forests and warm shores, and weave for your patient pictures of healing, beauty and tranquillity.

The voice is also a powerful healer, and yours is now directed by your higher guides.

❑ As the light and words flow, slowly move your hands from the crown chakra down to the patient's brow so your hands, palms outwards facing the patient, just cross in the centre of the patient's brow, 2 or 3 centimetres (about an inch) away from the skin.

❑ Hold your hands there as you continue to let the light flow and the words continue to paint wonderful realms, actual and magical.

❑ When you feel ready, move next to the centre of the throat and hold your hands, still palms outwards so one hand is in front of and touching the other, the same distance as before away from the patient's skin.

❑ Again, let light and words flow.

❑ Move next so your hands are in the centre of the patient's chest, maintaining the same distance away. This time form a horizontal curve with your hands, so your palms face outwards towards the patient as the words and light do their work.

❑ Finally, cup your hands over your patient's hands and ask them to open theirs so you can both again make connection with the crystals. You will feel the power ebbing away.

❏ Slowly remove your hands and sit talking quietly for a while.

❏ When you are ready, ask your patient to drop the crystals into a bowl of mineral water, where they too can rest and be restored.

❏ Thank the angels and wise guides for the power of light that has filled you with healing.

❏ Plunge your own hands into the bowl of water and shake them so water droplets fall from them.

9

A journey around the universe

At last we have reached the top two rungs on the cosmic ladder, the Anupadaka and the highest, the Adi plane, and we are operating through the outermost and most spiritually evolved layers of our aura.

Mystics who devote their lives to attaining a few moments of complete illumination and divine ecstasy have visited these planes in their visions. Mysticism is defined as an overwhelming sense of being in complete unity or oneness with the deity or cosmos, whether this is interpreted as a unity with the God, the Goddess or the Buddhist undifferentiated state of bliss, nirvana.

For the twelfth-century German mystic Hildegard of Bingen, her mystical experiences followed many years of gentle contemplation: 'And it came to pass, when I was 42 years and 7 months old, that the heavens were opened and a blinding light of exceptional brilliance flowed through my entire brain. And so it kindled my whole heart and breast like a flame, not burning but warming... And suddenly I understood of the meaning of the books.'

Those who withdraw from the world for a lifetime of meditation and contemplation may be able to work with guides on these highest levels, where the most elevated orders of angels – the thrones, the cherubim and seraphim – reside. The most important of these, the six-winged seraphim, guard the veil between the sixth plane and the final, unknowable level. Here too are the Holy family and various deity forms, who have been described as aspects of the God and Goddess in different religions and ages.

But for most of us there may be, in the midst of our busy lives, only moments of what the poet T S Eliot described as 'sudden in a shaft of sunlight ... costing not less than everything'. Yet such momentary glimpses of divinity can take away all fear of dying and of the power of evil. In the distance you may see the veil of mist and a fabulous golden light leading to pure divinity, in which everything is joined and resolved.

Talking to divinity

If you do want to work at these higher levels, you may decide to read about different religions and perhaps attend church services even if you are not a member of any particular faith. It may also be helpful to study ancient mythologies and the religion of other cultures and find gods and goddesses whose qualities seem to mirror the highest expression of those you most admire. There are many sites on the internet explaining religions in different cultures and their deity forms.

Perhaps you have not prayed privately since you were a child. T S Eliot described entry to cosmic unity as 'a moment of complete simplicity', and another poet, William Wordsworth, wrote about children being born 'trailing clouds of glory' and that 'heaven lies about us in our infancy'. As we get older, so we may lose the ease of divine connection and have to relearn it, often by following long spiritual pathways.

To regain that childlike sense of wonder and total trust, try the following ritual regularly.

First, find your place of personal religious sanctity, which might be at the end of the street or the other side of the world, a church or temple or a circle under the temple of the stars in a forest or on a shore. Some of the lovely old cathedrals can inspire those of many faiths or no specific one.

Choose a time when there is no one around and sunlight is softly filtering. Read some sacred literature or inspiring poetry or silently absorb the atmosphere of those who have come to worship here over the years.

Alternatively, wait until a choir is rehearsing or, as in some churches, sacred music is playing.

❐ Start talking, either softly aloud or in your mind. You need no script because, as you gain confidence, you will find yourself speaking honestly, openly and without fear of being judged or found lacking. Imagine you were talking to the kindest, wisest most perfect father or mother in the world.

❐ Wait when you have finished, not for an answer, but for a sense that your prayer is complete and has been accepted.

You may be rewarded by an unexpected shaft of sunlight, a vision in your mind of a place of incredible beauty or a feeling of deep peace not experienced since you went to sleep as a child after a particularly happy day.

❐ If you wish, open a Bible or prayer book that may be in the pew in front of you or use the sacred or inspiring literature you brought with you. Open it anywhere and begin reading as much or as little as you wish. You can be sure that the words will hold some answer from on high.

❏ Leave a flower or crystal outdoors or, if in a church or cathedral, light a candle for someone who needs healing and leave a small offering for the upkeep of the building.

Using peak experiences to reach these higher realms

It is also possible to approach these higher realms via a non-religious though spiritual route. The US psychologist Abraham Maslow was fascinated by mystical experiences. He believed that they were often based on what he called a 'peak experience' and could be secular as well as religious. He concluded that these moments of pure bliss and connection with the universe might occur only for a few seconds, but could be life-changing. The following are ways that people have experienced this sense of peak connection with what has been described as the heart of the universe.

Try one or two and you may experience total joy and release from the constraints of the conscious mind and truly soar in your spirit. Many are based in nature, but on a very high level. Recently, having interviewed people who have enjoyed peak experiences, I have been told of glimpses of heavenly realms, golden gates, angelic choirs and a sense of wonder and beauty that cannot be explained in words.

❏ Sit on a sunny shore or by a fountain in sunlight looking at the rippling water and allowing the sound to fill your mind.

❏ Listen to a choir, especially Gregorian chants in a cathedral as sunset filters through the windows, or buy a CD of choral music. The singing from the mountain-top monastery of Montserrat near Barcelona is truly celestial. If you can, try to hear the choir singing there.

❏ Watch the dawn rise over an ancient site at midsummer.

❏ Lie on the grass or a sun bed in the darkness and look up at the stars, focusing on one point and letting the others merge and dance so that the Milky Way appears to flow like a milky river of stars.

❏ Run downhill in a fierce wind, ride a horse along sand or through a forest, roll in snow, swim underwater among shoals of fish, or even through the illuminations of the pool lights at your local swimming baths.

❏ Splash through the path of moon or sunlight in the sea or the shallows of a lake, covering yourself with the radiance and singing at the top of your voice.

- ❏ Soothe a crying baby, whether your own or one you are taking care of for a friend or relative, and watch joy break through or the soft contented sigh as they drift into sleep.

- ❏ Blow bubbles from a children's bubble set from the top of a hill, fly a beautiful kite and let it go, to be found, hopefully, by a child, to whom it will give pleasure.

Travelling the universe

Now we are going to revisit the seven planes to explore more of the guides and the world they live in. There are many ways you can make this journey, some of which you have already met in the book. Ask your spirit guide and guardian angel to be with you, and at each level you will meet your other guides, who will walk with you and help you to move easily from one level to another.

Remember you are travelling only in your mind (or, some believe, your spirit, or etheric body). At any point you wish to return, thank your guides and slowly count down from twenty to zero. By zero you will be fully in the everyday world.

You can't get lost, because the everyday world intrudes sooner or later – perhaps through a child calling, someone walking close or a sudden chill. If there is an urgent need in the everyday world, the magical journey all too readily fades.

You may make the journey many times and each time you will experience something new. Keep a place in your journal for these wanderings, noting whom you meet and how you feel.

These experiences will explain or expand wisdom you have received from teachers and guides. I would advise you visit one or, at the most, two of the lower three realms at a session and generally no more than one of the higher realms.

Walking through the worlds

Once a week, or perhaps a fortnight, is enough for these astral wanderings on the lower planes, and if you find you are feeling tired, then leave this work for a while.

You can pass rapidly through the lower realms if you wish to visit higher ones on subsequent visits. You should only visit the higher planes, where the experiences are intense, once a month, and the highest planes two or three times a year, perhaps on a special date in your life.

Explore each of the lower spirit worlds at least once in preliminary sessions before moving on to the next one, even if you are experienced spiritually. When you do pass rapidly through a realm on your way to a higher one you may experience colours, lights and a feeling of moving through a light wind tunnel.

❏ You should begin by using one of the methods of psychic protection I suggest on pages 18–22, or surround yourself with a visualised bubble of light and ask for the protection of your guides and guardians. Your shadowy doorkeeper will wait at every level and if the time is not right he will gently turn you back.

Then either:

❏ Light a candle and walk through a doorway in a crystal sphere, a pyramid or geode.

❏ Look into a natural pool into which sunlight or moonlight shines and, like the shamans – the priest healers of indigenous people from Siberia to Africa – in your mind dive deep into the water and then swim into various caverns where there are paths leading to different realms. Though we talk about travelling upwards, in fact the different realms are all around us, just at far higher levels of vibration. The ladder idea can, however, be a helpful one.

❏ Stand beneath a tall tree and look up at the Pole Star or some other bright star. In your mind climb upwards in what the shamans of the northern hemisphere called 'the World Tree', or axis of the world, and continue climbing (see overleaf).

❏ Sit in the dark by the light of a fire or use incense sticks and create an upward pathway of smoke. The shamans used the smoke hole in the centre of their hut through which to travel in their minds.

❏ Listen to music, for example the music of dolphin calls or forest sounds, and ride on the sound on a beautiful, sleek, imaginary horse or panther.

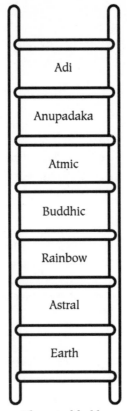

The astral ladder

☐ Focus on a candle or another light placed high on a shelf or on the ceiling in the corner of a room. Count from zero to twenty slowly in your mind and picture yourself walking up steps of light to and through the light, into the different planes.

☐ Lie on the grass on a sunny day when the bees are humming and the birds are singing and focus on a single cloud.

☐ Use a long journey in a plane to imagine walking on the fluffy clouds.

☐ On a long, high-speed train journey put on headphones to shut out the sound of people and watch the scenery fly by.

☐ Sit on the back of a ferry and in your mind float over the waves on a golden boat to different islands.

☐ Sit or lie in a tent or a hut in the wilderness as the rain is falling.

- Walk through a forest, or along a flat road where you can see for miles. Let your feet set the pace. Some of my best other-plane experiences were in city streets, pushing my insomniac children in their pushchairs in the evening to get them to sleep, while my own mind was exhausted.

- Travel in your dreams. Before sleep, create in your mind a signal of a very vivid symbol. For example, picture a butterfly and say:

> *When I see the huge multi-coloured butterfly in my dream I will know I am dreaming.*

Repeat the words and visualisation nightly before sleep till you do see the butterfly or your personal symbol in the dream. Once you know you are dreaming (called 'lucid dreaming'), you can fly, float, swim, climb, knowing that you are quite safe because this is your dream and you can change any aspects that worry you, overcome any dragons in the mythical lands and know your guardians are always close.

The seven planes and the coloured rays

The different colours associated with the spiritual levels of the aura (see Chapter 5) are also sometimes applied to the corresponding planes.

However, some philosophical systems link specific coloured rays of radiance with the seven planes. These are the colours through which you may identify each plane, perhaps as a swirling mist that suddenly clears. Each plane will be suffused with light of the most beautiful shade of its own colour you can imagine.

The seven rays of radiance and their various associations are quite complex and inevitably conflicting when filtered through human experience. Writing about this concept would fill several books. If you are interested there are numerous sites on the internet. Enter 'Seven Rays' on the web browser and be prepared for a lot of differing accounts. Choose what feels right for you. If you already work through a healing tradition, you will have your own system through which these rays are conceptualised. However, you may see a golden light for all of them, and your vision is as valid as anyone's.

These are the most common colours associated with the seven planes. I have also listed the fragrances associated with each plane, which you can burn as incense sticks if you wish, or use the flowers or any form of the fragrance.

The Earth (Etheric) plane

Ray: Violet.

Fragrances: Lilac or strawberry.

Here, as the mists clear, your spirit guide will be waiting, as will your spirit physician and life-skills teacher. Take the time to talk to them and ask any questions face to face. Though they do not live here, they will have created homes, workshops and surgeries, better than the very best on Earth, where you can meet.

Here you can see or visit other earthly lands by focusing on specific places and walking through gateways or flying across the sky holding on to your spirit guide, who will not let you fall. This realm is what people experience when they talk of out-of-body travel.

You can talk mind to mind to friends and relatives who live far away, and visit their homes if they invite you. Afterwards you will be surprised when you write or phone, how accurate the pictures were. Or you can explore the beautiful gardens, forests and buildings and marvel at the most perfect flowers, trees and species of birds, animals and butterflies.

If you lie down and sleep for a while here, you may also see your other wise guardians and your guardian angel, who are waiting on the higher planes.

You have the option to return to the everyday world or go on. Your personal guide will be with you.

The Astral (Emotional) plane

Ray: Rose.

Fragrances: Carnation or myrrh.

This is the most magical of lands and one you may wish to return to many times. You may recall it from your childhood, but it also runs deeper. This is the realm visited by shamans to obtain healing for individuals and to negotiate with the mistresses of the herds or the sea creatures to release the creatures to the hunting grounds.

Though your spirit guide will be at your side, many of the fairy folk and the nature spirits may take their time to approach you. Be patient and remember you are the visitor.

Here also are the chiefs of the wise animals whose wisdom the Native North Americans valued so much. They will, if you are quiet and wait to be approached, be welcoming, and their wisdom is to be treasured.

Walk further, perhaps on a subsequent visit, and you will realise there are not only animal species you recognise but mythical creatures, magical birds, unicorns, phoenixes and all those species that have become extinct on Earth. Here, if you suspend belief, you may encounter magical forests and birds and creatures whose words are translated into human language.

Be guided by your spirit guardian, especially if you see caves or huts in the forest. Here may reside the ancient mothers of the herds and, in deep, watery caverns, the sea mothers, who control the shoals of fish. If you are allowed to see into one of these dwellings, be silent and follow your guide. For in this realm are all the ideas and thoughts in their archetypal or idealised form that you have read about in mythology and which lie behind all the great systems of philosophy and psychology.

In what seems like a giant fairy story, you may encounter the wise woman, the adventurer, the trickster, the great ruler, the healer, the hero, the dreamer and the talking animal who represents your own instinctive wisdom. As you talk to these characters and watch scenes unfold, you will realise they represent aspects and qualities within yourself. By watching their interactions, you will learn a lot about yourself and your earthly path and relationships.

This is a good plane to visit through lucid dreams. Your helper guides and your personal spirit guide will assist you to interpret this plane and to use your experiences positively.

You can now go back or go on, but there is plenty of time, so don't overwhelm yourself with experiences. Visiting other planes is mentally and spiritually demanding.

131

The Rainbow (Mental) plane

Ray: Orange.

Fragrances: Lily or mint.

This is akin to our idea of heaven and is where your family and wise ancestors live. It is said they fashion from their thoughts the kind of lives they wish to live, right down to their homes. To the Ancient Egyptians, this realm was the 'Blessed Field of Reeds', situated in the Milky Way, to the Celts the 'Isles of the Blest' and to Spiritualists 'Summerland' or 'the Summerlands'.

This too is a realm you may visit spontaneously during sleep. More dramatically, people may enter it temporarily during in a near-death experience, where access has been described as travelling down a tunnel towards a point of light.

Here you will experience a sensation like looking through a huge glass screen and see the scenes of the afterlife most personal to you. You may hear beautiful music and see wonderful flowers that might form carpets. Colours will be brighter than earthly colours and all your senses will be heightened.

You may see your relatives, young and fit, and their homes or workplaces, and one of them may see you looking in and wave. If you are lucky, your deceased grandmother or grandfather will appear by your side and hug you and you can share family news. He or she will give you advice and reassurance and perhaps point out one or two things you ought to be doing to maintain important family contact. They may describe their new life and perhaps allow you to momentarily glimpse it through their eyes.

Your personal ancestor may appear and show you his world, perhaps more than a hundred years earlier, for time has no meaning here. He too will talk and encourage you.

Finally, you may encounter your spiritual ancestor, who might take you to Ancient Egypt, the world of the Vikings or an ancient temple and help you to understand why you are fascinated by a particular place and time in history.

You will see nothing disturbing or frightening, nor will you witness illness or death, because they just do not exist here.

Gradually this realm will fade and you may feel sleepy. Let go and your spirit guide will take you back to the everyday world, as you may be too tired to travel further. But you can always return later.

The Buddhic (Astral) plane

Ray: Yellow.

Fragrances: Rose or thyme.

The realms are becoming progressively mistier and less substantial and now you will be seeing not through glass, but through coloured light. Your guardian angel will be waiting and you will feel the softness of his wings and hear the clear voice you have heard so many times in your mind.

There will be temples, altars, shrines and an overwhelming sense of fragrance quite unlike earthly fragrances. You will hear music more beautiful than the most wonderful choir on Earth, and experience such a sense of lightness you feel you could easily float away. Indeed the bottom of the plane may be covered with clouds so that you are not sure if the figures you see are walking, floating or flying.

There will be huge, marble libraries filled with knowledge, some of it from the advanced civilisations of Atlantis and Lemuria that according to myth, disappeared under the sea and were lost to humanity.

Through the mist will come spirit guides who either have never lived or are wise mortals who have decided to devote themselves after life to teaching and guiding humans on Earth. Among them will be those teachers who have offered to guide you and teach you about healing or spirituality. Their faces will be filled with light. Other people may be standing in the mist waiting as you are and their guides will pick them out and lead them to a special temple or library.

This plane may be the home of your spirit guide, or he or she may choose to live on the Rainbow plane, depending on their own stage of spiritual evolution. One day you may go and see through human eyes the place your personal guide calls home. But for now one of your wise teachers will take you into one of the buildings and perhaps allow you to look into a book of lost wisdom. The experience will be dreamlike and, suddenly, as you reach out to read a page in one of the great books, the mists will close round it. But afterwards you will understand missing connections in conventional knowledge.

Your guardian angel will touch you with the special signal you have. Your spirit guide will take you, like an exhausted child, back to the place on Earth where you began this exploration.

133

The Atmic (Etheric) plane

Ray: Green.

Fragrances: Lavender or mimosa.

On the Atmic plane, silver light may shine through the green mists and you will be aware of wonderful golden beings: archangels, saints and pillars of light that swirl rather than walk or float. This is a realm of pure energy. You will view this plain from a great distance, perhaps on a hilltop. Around you will dance light-beams and rainbows and your angel and spirit guide will hold your hands so that they can absorb some of the energies and you will not be overwhelmed.

Ahead of you on the golden plain will be one beautiful, dazzling building that seems to be made of pure light, a building so huge that even from far away you cannot see the top of its pillars.

Your spirit guide will ask if you would like to see the Akashic records housed within its halls. These records hold all human experience, past, present and future, so do not ask to see them until you feel ready. Some people never want to.

But if you do ask to see what lies on your page, you will become aware of another presence that you may see as a column of silver, who is one of your higher guides or teachers or one of the guardians of the records, light beings who will not speak. You will probably not learn the identity of your guide.

Your spirit guide and guardian angel will step back because they do not have the power to take you into the Akashic halls, though they will still protect you. The higher being will enfold you in warm light and, through what seems like a doorway in this light, you will find yourself looking at a dazzling book and at your personal page.

Here you can read of your past lives and future opportunities. Be assured that the day of your earthly death is the one thing you will not be allowed to see, nor should you seek to, for such matters are known only to the highest divine powers (and are affected by many factors).

Then the light will fade and your spirit guide and angel will carry you gently, as though you were a baby, back to the everyday world where you began the experience. You will feel as though you are waking from a long sleep, so take your time. You will not recall much, but as you return to that realm more details will become etched in your memory that can be retrieved in sleep or quiet times.

Do not visit this plane more than once a month, and try to spend time on the lower planes to keep your perspective and the channels open.

The Anupadaka (Celestial) plane

Rays: Blue or indigo.

Fragrances: Sandalwood or sage.

This a remarkably still plane where all you may see is an unadorned altar or shrine of pure gold and, all round it, radiance. This will be so bright that though you are at a great distance, even through the blue or indigo ray, you can only glimpse it for a second without hurting your eyes. Your spirit guide and guardian angel will be just behind you, telling you that you cannot stay and must turn away.

Before you turn, look towards the altar and see your very personal view of divinity. It may be a form you recognise from church paintings or mythology, or it may be altogether less defined but incredibly beautiful. At this moment you will feel the divine spark within your soul kindle and flare and you will know you are blessed and need not fear anything.

Then the scene will be lost in blue or indigo mist so dense you have to hold your guide's and angel's hands to find the way back. But they will not stumble, and with your new-found trust you know that this is a very special moment in your life.

Only repeat this perhaps two or three times a year and each time the glimpse of divinity will be clearer and more wonderful.

The Adi (Ketheric) plane

Rays: Red or gold.

Fragrances: Frankincense or lotus.

One day, just before you leave the Anupadaka plane, your spirit guide or guardian angel may step back and a huge, radiant being of light may pass his star-like fingers in front of your eyes. Just for a second you will glimpse a vast, star-studded veil, through which shines radiance you can perceive only through half-closed eyes.

That is the threshold to the Adi plane. You may become momentarily aware of huge six-winged beings on your side of the veil, the seraphim, whose heads disappear into the clouds, though you are what seems miles away. At this point your heart will be touched from within and you may want to laugh, cry, pray and sing all at the same time. You may hear a crescendo of celestial voices and feel great warmth and become aware that you too are bathed in light. Then there will be total silence, utter peace, and your spirit guide and guardian angel will lead you back in silence through the mists of the Anupadaka plane.

You will not experience this every time, nor should you seek to, but perhaps it will occur a few times during your lifetime. These experiences increase as we become older, and what is more, it is said that on the point of death we glimpse the glory of the seventh plane and so can walk with joy into eternity.

Useful materials for spirit-guide work

Crystals

The materials listed include the key ones featured in the text and some others you may find useful.

Crystal	Description	Door-keeper	Protective	Sleep channelling	Angelic communication	Earth	Air	Fire	Water	Arch-angel
Agate, black	Black		✓			✓				
Agate, blood	Red glowing							✓		
Agate, blue lace	Pale blue						✓			
Agate, fire	Red-brown							✓		
Agate, moss	Green					✓				
Agate, tree	Dark green					✓				
Amazonite	Mid-green					✓				
Amber	Golden orange		✓					✓		✓
Amethyst	Lilac	✓	✓	✓	✓		✓			✓
Ametrine	Purple/ golden yellow		✓	✓	✓				✓	
Angelite	Soft blue and opaque, veined with wings				✓		✓			
Aqua aura	Transparent electric blue				✓		✓			

Crystal	Description	Door-keeper	Protective	Sleep channelling	Angelic communication	Earth	Air	Fire	Water	Arch-angel
Aquamarine	Transparent, turquoise blue		✓	✓					✓	
Aura, cobalt titanium	Brilliant royal blue, violet and gold			✓	✓					✓
Aura, opal	Translucent white that shimmers with rainbows			✓	✓					✓
Aventurine	Mottled pale green					✓				
Azurite	Dark blue/indigo wqith iridescent flashes		✓		✓		✓			✓
Golden Beryl	Transparent to translucent yellow-green				✓			✓		✓
Bloodstone	Green with red markings		✓					✓		
Boji stones	Dark brown grey							✓		
Calcite	Orange/yellow								✓	
Carnelian	Dark orange glowing		✓					✓		✓

Crystal	Description	Door-keeper	Protective	Sleep channelling	Angelic communication	Earth	Air	Fire	Water	Arch-angel
Celestite	Semi-transparent blue, like ice				✓	✓				
Chalcedony, blue	Opaque and soft blue		✓		✓		✓			
Chrysopras	Opaque apple green				✓				✓	✓
Citrine	Orange-yellow						✓			✓
Coral	Pink/red		✓						✓	
Crystal sphere or pyramid	Any crystal pyramid or small crystal sphere	✓	✓		✓	✓				✓
Danburite	Clear, quartz-like				✓		✓			
Desert rose	Sand-coloured		✓				✓	✓		
Diamond	Clear and sparkling				✓		✓			✓
Emerald	Green		✓		✓	✓				✓
Fluorite	Purple or green			✓	✓				✓	
Fossils	Stone		✓			✓				
Garnet	Transparent red		✓					✓		
Goldstone, blue	Blue with gold			✓	✓		✓			✓
Hematite	Grey shiny		✓					✓		✓

Crystal	Description	Door-keeper	Protective	Sleep channelling	Angelic communication	Earth	Air	Fire	Water	Arch-angel
Herkimer diamond	Clear and shiny		✓		✓		✓			✓
Iron pyrites	Gold and shiny		✓					✓		
Isis crystal	Clear quartz with five edges surrounding the largest sloping face	✓			✓		✓			
Jade	Green		✓		✓				✓	✓
Jasper, black	Black and dark brown and russet striped		✓					✓		
Jasper, red	Dark brown and russet striped		✓					✓		
Jasper, yellow	Yellow							✓		✓
Jet	Black	✓	✓			✓				
Kunzite	Pinky-white				✓				✓	
Lapis lazuli	Rich dark blue with gold flecks		✓		✓		✓			✓

Crystal	Description	Door-keeper	Protective	Sleep channelling	Angelic communication	Earth	Air	Fire	Water	Arch-angel
Laser crystal	Clear crystal quartz with seven edges surrounding the large sloping face	✓	✓		✓		✓			✓
Lava	Grey		✓					✓		
Lepidolite	Pearlescent light purple	✓	✓		✓				✓	
Malachite	Green striped		✓			✓				
Moonstone	Translucent, creamy			✓	✓				✓	✓
Obsidian	Black and shiny		✓					✓		✓
Opal	Rainbow shimmering		✓	✓	✓				✓	✓
Pearl	Opaque gleaming		✓	✓	✓				✓	✓
Quartz, channelling or laser	Seven edges surrounding the large sloping face	✓			✓		✓			✓
Quartz, clear crystal	Clear, glassy				✓		✓			✓
Quartz, milky	White		✓	✓					✓	✓

Crystal	Description	Door-keeper	Protective	Sleep channelling	Angelic communi-cation	Earth	Air	Fire	Water	Arch-angel
Quartz, phantom	A small crystal within a larger host	✓			✓		✓			✓
Quartz, rainbow	With prismatic fractures that create rainbows when they catch the light		✓		✓		✓			✓
Quartz, rose	Pink		✓	✓	✓	✓				✓
Quartz, rutilated	Clear with gleaming gold strands		✓		✓	✓				✓
Quartz, smoky	Semi-transparent dark grey-brown	✓	✓			✓				
Quartz, spirit	Covered with tiny crystals				✓		✓			✓
Ruby	Dark red	✓	✓	✓	✓			✓		✓
Sapphire	Blue		✓		✓		✓			✓
Selenite	Semi-transparent or satin striped		✓	✓	✓				✓	✓
Sodalite	Indigo or deep blue	✓	✓	✓			✓			
Suglite	Purple			✓	✓		✓			✓

Crystal	Description	Door-keeper	Protective	Sleep channelling	Angelic communication	Earth	Air	Fire	Water	Arch-angel
Tiger's eye	Dark brown and orange striped		✓		✓	✓				✓
Topaz	Clear or orange brown, yellow or blue		✓		✓			✓		✓
Tourmaline	Pink, green, blue, black		✓	✓					✓	
Turquoise	Turquoise		✓		✓		✓			✓
Wood, petrified	Mottled and brown striped	✓	✓			✓				

Herbs and fragrances

The materials listed include the key ones featured in the text and some others you may find useful.

Herb or fragrance	Description of aroma	Protective	Earth	Air	Fire	Water
Acacia (Acacia)	Warm, sweet, spicy and floral	✓		✓	✓	
Allspice (Calycanthus floridus)	Spicy, cinnamon-nutmeg-clove				✓	
Almond (Prunus dulcis var. amara)	Sweet almond, lightly floral			✓		
Angelica (Angelica archangelica)	Fresh and peppery				✓	
Anise (Pimpinella anisum)	Sweet liquorice	✓		✓		
Apple blossom (Pyrus malus)	Fruity, floral and sweet	✓				✓
Apricot (Prunus armeniaca)	Sweet and fruity with a hint of plum					✓
Basil (Ocimum basilicum)	Sweet herbaceous	✓			✓	
Bay (Laurus nobilis)	Slightly aniseed	✓			✓	
Benzoin (Styrax benzoin)	Sweet vanilla			✓		
Bergamot (Citrus bergamia)	Orange and slightly woody			✓		
Carnation (Dianthus caryophyllus)	Heavy floral	✓			✓	
Cedarwood (Juniper virginiana, Cedrus atlantica)	Warm and woody	✓			✓	
Chamomile (Chamaemelum nobile, Matricaria recutitao)	Sweet, honeyed herbaceous				✓	
Cinnamon (Cinnamomum cassia)	Rich and spicy				✓	

Herb or fragrance	Description of aroma	Protective	Earth	Air	Fire	Water
Clove (Eugenia caryophyllata)	Warm, sweet and spicy				✓	
Coconut	Coconut, sweet, toasted					✓
Copal	Spicy and uplifting	✓			✓	
Cypress (Cupressus sempervirens)	Spicy, resinous pine	✓	✓			
Dill (Anethum graveolens)	Warm, spicy, caraway and spearmint	✓		✓		
Dragon's-blood	Oriental sharp, orange and rose	✓			✓	
Eucalyptus (Eucalyptus globulus)	Powerful, distinctive					✓
Fennel (Foeniculum vulgare)	Aniseed			✓		
Fern	Fresh, green		✓			
Feverfew (Tanacetum perthenium)	Bitter camphor					
Frankincense (Boswellia carterii)	Spicy and peppery	✓			✓	✓
Geranium (Pelargonium graveolens)	Sweet, refreshing and floral	✓	✓			
Grasses	Sweet and green			✓		
Heather (Calluna vulgaris)	Sweet and floral		✓			
Heliotrope (Heliotropium peruviana)	Sweet, mild and floral	✓			✓	✓
Hibiscus (Hibiscus rosa-sinensis)	Fresh, green and slightly musky	✓	✓			
Honeysuckle (Lonicera chrysantha)	Fresh and sweet	✓	✓			
Hyacinth (Hyacinth orientalis)	Fresh, sweet and floral	✓	✓			✓
Jasmine (Jasminum grandiflorum)	Honey floral, slightly woody	✓				✓

Herb or fragrance	Description of aroma	Protective	Earth	Air	Fire	Water
Juniper (Juniperus communis)	Warm and slightly woody	✓			✓	
Lavender (Lavandula angustifolia)	Clean, floral and slightly woody	✓		✓		
Lemon (Citrus limonum)	Lemon					✓
Lemon balm (Melissa officinalis)	Sharp and lemony					✓
Lemon verbena (Aloysia triphylla)	Lemon and camphor			✓		
Lemongrass (Cymbopogen citratus)	Sweet, sharp and lemony	✓		✓		
Lilac (Syringa vulgaris)	Strong floral and sweet	✓				✓
Lily (Lilium)	Floral	✓				✓
Lily of the valley (Convallaria majalis)	Sweet and strong			✓		
Lime (Tilia)	Refreshing lime				✓	✓
Lotus	Rich, heady					
Magnolia (Magnolia glauca)	Floral rose	✓	✓			
Marigold (Tagetes minuta)	Fruity, herbal and slightly bitter				✓	
Marjoram (Origanum marjorana)	Sweet, spicy and herbal	✓		✓		
Meadowsweet (Filipendula ulmaria)	Green, astringent		✓	✓		
Mimosa	Rich, floral	✓				
Myrrh (Commiphora myrrha)	Rich and resinous	✓				✓
Nettle (Urtica dioica)	Fresh and green	✓			✓	

Herb or fragrance	Description of aroma	Protective	Earth	Air	Fire	Water
Nutmeg (Myristica fragrans)	Rich and spicy				✓	
Oakmoss (Evernia prunasti)	Woody, earthy with a touch of tar	✓	✓			
Orange blossom (Citrus aurantium sinensis)	Orange, sweet and fresh	✓			✓	
Orchid (Orchis)	Green and herbal	✓				✓
Papyrus flower (Cyperus papyrus)	Mentholated	✓		✓		
Passionflower (Passiflora caerulea)	Sweet, fruity and floral					✓
Patchouli (Pogostemon patchouli)	Musty and woody		✓			
Peach (Prunus persica)	Fruity peach					✓
Peppermint (Mentha piperata)	Fresh and minty	✓		✓		
Pine (Pinus)	Resinous pine	✓			✓	
Rose (Rosa damascena)	Rose, fresh and sweet	✓				✓
Rosemary (Rosmarinus officinalis)	Strong herbaceous mix of lavender and camphor	✓			✓	
Sage (Salvia lavendulafolia)	Herbal, slightly musky	✓	✓	✓		
Sagebrush (Artemisia tridentata)	Sweet and pungent	✓	✓			
Sandalwood (Santalum album)	Sweet and woody	✓		✓		
Strawberry (Fragaria ananassa)	Strawberry fruit, sweet and ripe					✓
Sweet pea (Lathyrus odoratus)	Delicate and lilacy					✓
Sweetgrass (Hierochloe odorata)	Grassy and fresh	✓	✓			

Herb or fragrance	Description of aroma	Protective	Earth	Air	Fire	Water
Tangerine (Citrus nobilis)	Sharp orange				✓	
Thyme (Thymus vulgaris)	Strong, fresh and green	✓				✓
Valerian (Valeriana officinalis)	Warm and woody					✓
Vanilla (Trilisa odoratissima)	Sweet, floral and vanilla	✓				✓
Vervain (Verbena officinalis)	Slightly bitter, astringent	✓	✓			
Vetivert (Vetiveria zizanioides)	Rich, sweet and earthy	✓	✓			
Violet (Viola odorata)	Sweet, floral and violet	✓				✓

Spirits

Element	Key Crystals	Materials	Fragrances	Colours
Earth	Most agates, amazonite, aventurine, emerald, fossils, jet, malachite, rose quartz, rutilated quartz, smoky quartz, tiger's eye, petrified wood, all stones with holes in the centre	Salt, soil, herbs, flowers, trees, coins, milk, beer, honey, fruit, nuts and seeds, pot-pourri, pot plants, earth, soil or grass, forest- or animal-call music	Cypress, fern, geranium, heather, hibiscus, honeysuckle, magnolia, oakmoss, patchouli, sagebrush, sweetgrass, vervain, vetivert	Green and brown
Air	Blue lace agate, amethyst, clear crystal quartz, citrine, danburite, diamond, lapis lazuli, sapphire, sodalite, sugilite, turquoise	Feathers, feathery grasses, ceiling mobiles, wind chimes, fragrances and fragrance sprays, open windows, clouds, mist, bird-call music	Acacia, almond, anise, benzoin, bergamot, dill, fennel, lavender, lemon verbena, lemongrass, lily of the valley, marjoram, meadowsweet, papyrus flower, peppermint, sage	Yellow and grey

Element	Key Crystals	Materials	Fragrances	Colours
Fire	Blood and fire agate, amber, bloodstone, boji stones, carnelian, desert rose, garnet, hematite, iron pyrites, jasper, lava, obsidian, ruby, topaz.	Lights of all kinds, especially fibre optic lamps, sun catchers, crystal spheres of all kinds that reflect rainbows, essential oils, natural sunshine, rain-oranges and all orange bows, fruit, sunflowers and all golden or orange flowers, music from hot lands, anything gold	Allspice, angelica, basil, bay, carnation, cedarwood, chamomile, cinnamon, cloves, copal, dragon's-blood, frankincense, heliotrope, juniper, lime, marigold, nutmeg, orange, rosemary, tangerine	Gold, orange and red
Water	Aquamarine, calcite, coral, fluorite, jade, kunzite, moonstone, opal, pearl, milky quartz, selenite, and tourmaline	Milk, water, sea shells, kelp, water features, nets or webs, dreamcatchers, fish in tanks, sea creature and dolphin images, silk scarves, transparent drapes, silver bells on cords, silver or copper items, silver foil, sea, river or dolphin music	Apple blossom, apricot, coconut, eucalyptus, feverfew, hyacinth, jasmine, lemon, lemon balm, lilac, lily, myrrh, orchid, passionflower, peach, strawberry, sweet pea, thyme, valerian, vanilla, violet	Blue and silver

151

Archangels

Angel	Direction	Element	Colour	Planet	Key Crystals	Incenses	Day	Symbol
Uriel	North	Earth	Red or scarlet	Mars	Amber, carnelian, rutilated quartz and tiger's eye	Sandalwood or rosemary, bay and copal	Tuesday	
Raphael	East	Air	Yellow	Mercury	Yellow calcite, golden beryl, citrine and yellow jasper	Fern, lavender mint, pine	Wednesday	
Michael	South	Fire	Gold	Sun	Amber, carnelian, clear quartz crystal and golden topaz	Chamomile, frankincense, marigold, rosemary and sage	Sunday	
Gabriel	West	Water	Silver	Moon	Moonstone, opals, pearls, milky quartz, selenite	Jasmine, lilac, mimosa, myrrh and rose	Monday	

Index